THE EFFECTIVE CISSP

SECURITY AND RISK MANAGEMENT

First Edition

Wentz Wu

The Effective CISSP
Security and Risk Management

Published by Wentz Wu (https://WentzWu.com)

ISBN: 978-957-43-7647-6

Cover Designer: CHING I.HSU

DEDICATION

To my father, for teaching me integrity;
To my mother, for nursing me kindness.

ACKNOWLEDGMENTS

I would like to express my sincerest thanks to my friends, Aaron, Daniel, Pato, Steve, and Tac, for supporting me all the time.

Special thanks go to Dr. Sunrise Chen and Jordan Dong for your mentoring and guidance to the CISSP community and cybersecurity markets.

Thanks to Ethan Chan, Fadi Sodah, and Sven De Preter for reviewing this book.

Thanks to Chaudhary Darvin for your valuable time and insightful feedback and suggestions.

Thanks to members of my Facebook group - Effective CISSP and many others who provided support and contacted me with information, inquiries, suggestions, and corrections.

Thanks to the following Facebook groups for accepting me and advancing the profession:

- CISSP Exam Preparation - Study Notes and Theory
- CISSP, CISM and PMP certification training by Thor Teaches!
- Get CISSP Certified
- Information Audit
- CISSP Master Class
- CISSP Certification Group
- CISSP Study Group

This book would not have been possible without your support and assistance.

Warmest regards,
Wentz Wu

PREFACE

I wrote this book as an attempt to propose an integral conceptual model for security by integrating ISO 31000, NIST FARM Risk Framework, and PMI Organizational Project Management (OPM) Framework to provide a holistic view for CISSP aspirants.

Traditionally, **risk** implies bad or negative things. **Threats** are intuitively related to risk, because of the implication of loss, unsafe, or insecure. It is common for security professionals to perceive them as related but confused. Moreover, various risk management approaches and inconsistent definitions of risk terminologies make it worse.

On the other hand, there are few tutorial materials on issues of **security governance**, such as strategic management, policy development, and program management. CISSP aspirants have to refer to MBA courses and PMI OPM framework for details, that rely on adequate work experience for good comprehension. It can be a challenge for some CISSP aspirants.

This book proposes two overarching models as the guidance for the first CISSP Domain: Wentz's Risk and Governance Model. **Wentz's Risk Model** is based on the concept of neutral risk and integrates the Peacock Model, the Onion Model, and the Protection Ring Model derived from the NIST Generic Risk Model. **Wentz's Governance Model** is a derivative of the integral discipline of governance, risk management, and compliance (GRC).

Last but not least, this book includes the **Amicliens InfoSec Conceptual Model** as the blueprint for all the eight CISSP domains. I hope this book helps in understanding the core concepts of the *CISSP Domain 1 – Security and Risk Management*.

ABOUT THE AUTHOR

Wentz Wu is the co-founder of Amicliens and has been working in the IT industry for more than 20 years. He is devoted to applying information technologies to solve business problems, delivering training and education courses, and giving back to the community.

In his professional career, Wentz is skilled at implementing IT infrastructure and cloud services, developing quality software, conducting comprehensive business analysis, managing projects with agility, and advising and delivering practical business solutions.

With a solid technical background and business savvy, Wentz comprehensively offers the CISSP course based on the *Amicliens InfoSec Conceptual Model*, which effectively addresses the official (ISC)² CISSP exam outline.

As a lifelong learner, Wentz demonstrates his endeavor and achievement as follows:
- EMBA/CBAP/PMP/ACP/PBA/RMP
- CGEIT/CISM/CRISC/CISA
- CISSP-ISSMP,ISSEP,ISSAP/CCSP/CSSLP
- CEH/ECSA/AWS-CSAA/MCSD/MCSE/MCDBA
- SCRUM: PSM Level I/PSPO Level I/PSD Level I
- ISO 27001 LA/ISO 27701 LA Courses Completed

Wentz can be reached through:
Email: wentzwu@gmail.com
Blog: https://WentzWu.com
Facebook: https://www.facebook.com/groups/EffectiveCISSP
YouTube: https://www.youtube.com/c/EffectiveCISSP

CONTENTS

List of Figures

List of Tables

xviii   CONTENTS

1 INTRODUCTION TO CISSP

"Time utilization and effectiveness is a major marker for success."

- Sunday Adelaja

1.1 HOW TO USE THIS BOOK

1.1.1 THE AUDIENCE OF THIS BOOK

This book is for CISSP aspirants and those who are interested in information security or confused by cybersecurity buzzwords and jargon. It is a supplement, not a replacement, to the CISSP study guides that CISSP aspirants have used as their primary source.

This book introduces core concepts, not all topics, of Domain 1 in the CISSP CBK - Security and Risk Management. It helps CISSP aspirants build a conceptual security model or blueprint so that they can proceed to read other materials, learn confidently and with less frustration, and pass the CISSP exam accordingly.

1.1.2 ORGANIZATION OF THIS BOOK

There are six chapters in this book organized structurally and sequenced logically. If you are new to CISSP, read them in sequence; if you are eager to learn anything and have a bird view from one thousand feet high, the author highly suggests keeping an eye on <u>Chapter 2 Security and Risk Management</u>.

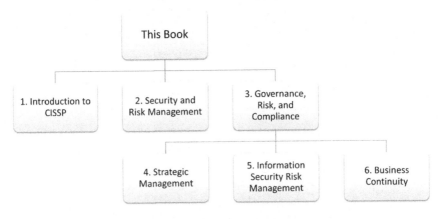

FIGURE 1-1 ORGANIZATION OF THIS BOOK

1.2 (ISC)² AND CISSP

With the vision to "**inspire a safe and secure cyber world**", the International Information System Security Certification Consortium, or **(ISC)²**, founded in 1989 and based in Florida, has been recognized as the world's leading cybersecurity professional organization. Its founders and members have been advancing the information security profession since then.

Cybersecurity Certifications

Many cybersecurity professional organizations administer certification programs. **(ISC)²**, **ISACA** (Information Systems Audit and Control Association), and **EC-Council** are some of them, and (ISC)² is the first information security certifying body to meet the requirements of ANSI/ISO/IEC Standard 17024.

This book categorizes cybersecurity certifications into **governance, management**, and **operations**. (The governance level refers to the **board of directors** and the **executive management**.)

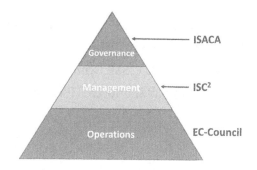

FIGURE 1-2 CYBERSECURITY CERTIFICATION CATEGORIES

However, GIAC (Global Information Assurance Certification), CompTIA (Computing Technology Industry Association), and many other well-known certification providers and professional organizations are not depicted in the diagram.

1.2.1   (ISC)² CERTIFICATION PROGRAMS

(ISC)² information security certifications are recognized as the global standard for excellence.

The following are the (ISC)² Certification Programs:

1. Certified Information Systems Security Professional (CISSP)
2. Information Systems Security Architecture Professional (CISSP-ISSAP)
3. Information Systems Security Engineering Professional (CISSP-ISSEP)
4. Information Systems Security Management Professional (CISSP-ISSMP)
5. Certified Secure Software Lifecycle Professional (CSSLP)
6. Certified Authorization Professional (CAP)
7. Certified Cloud Security Professional (CCSP)
8. Systems Security Certified Practitioner (SSCP)
9. HealthCare Information Security and Privacy Practitioner (HCISPP)

ISSEP, ISSAP, and ISSMP are CISSP concentration certifications that are available to CISSPs only. The author considers ISSEP and ISSAP are extensions to CISSP Domain 3, ISSMP is the extension to CISSP Domain 1, and CSSLP is the extension to CISSP Domain 8.

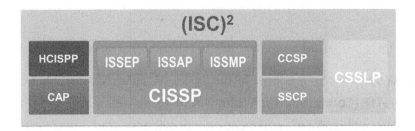

FIGURE 1-3 (ISC)² CERTIFICATION PROGRAMS

1.2.2   DoD Directive 8570.1-M

Certified Information Systems Security Professional (CISSP) is the world's premier cybersecurity certification. CISSP is a security certification that focuses on information systems. It meets the requirements of the DoD Directive 8570.1-M.

The U.S. Department of Defense (DoD) Directive 8140.01, "Cyberspace Workforce Management," on August 11, 2015, superseded DoD Directive 8570.01. However, the DoD Directive 8570.01-M governing the IA workforce certification program is still in effect.

The following table lists only some of the DoD Directive 8570.1 approved baseline certifications.

IAT Level I	IAT Level II	IAT Level III
A+	Security+	CISA
Network+	GSEC	CISSP
SSCP	GICSP	GCED
	SSCP	GCIH
		GICSP

IAM Level I	IAM Level II	IAM Level III
GSLC	GSLC	GSLC
CAP	CISM	CISM
Security+	CISSP	CISSP
	CAP	

IASAE Level I	IASAE Level II	IASAE Level III
CISSP	CISSP	CISSP-ISSAP
CSSLP	CSSLP	CISSP-ISSEP

Computer Network Defense-Service Provider (CND-SP)				
Analyst	Infrastructure Support	Incident Responder	Auditor	SP Manager
CEH	CEH	CEH	CEH	CISSP-ISSMP
GCIA	SSCP	GCFA	CISA	CISM
GCIH	GICSP	GCIH	GSNA	
GICSP				

FIGURE 1-4 DOD 8570.1 BASELINE CERTIFICATIONS

Information Assurance (IA)

- Information Assurance Technical (IAT)
- Information Assurance Management (IAM)

CISSP covers all the positions at all levels in IAT and IAM.

IA System Architect and Engineer (IASAE)

- System Architect (SA)
- System Engineer (SE)

CISSP meets the requirements of level II at most. Only CISSP-ISSAP or CISSP-ISSEP meets the requirements of level III in the category of ISAAE.

Computer Network Defense Service Provider (CND-SP)

- Computer Network Defense Analyst (CND-A)
- Computer Network Defense Infrastructure Support (CND-IS)
- Computer Network Defense Incident Responder (CND-IR)
- Computer Network Defense Auditor (CND-AU)
- Computer Network Defense Service Provider Manager (CND-SPM)

CEH covers most of the positions in the category of CND-SP. However, only CISSP-CISM or CISM meets the requirements of the service provider manager.

Please visit the "Cyber Workforce Management Program" for details. (https://public.cyber.mil/cwmp)

1.2.3   CYBERSECURITY CAREER ROADMAP

CISSP is acclaimed as the gold standard of the security industry. As the comprehensiveness of certification requirements, individuals are considered experienced and knowledgeable information security professionals once certified as CISSP.

CISSP plays a strategic and central role in security certifications. It builds a solid foundation to extend career path to **security governance, security management, security operations,** and other specialty security areas such as **cloud security, software security,** and **infrastructure security.**

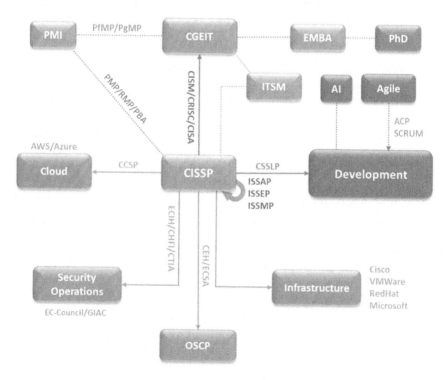

FIGURE 1-5 THE STRATEGIC ROLE OF CISSP

Security Management

- CISSP covers both **management** and **technical** concepts. It is comprehensive and builds a solid foundation for other certifications.
- ISSAP, ISSEP, and ISSMP are **CISSP Concentrations**; they are extensions to CISSP in terms of architecture, engineering, and management and available for CISSPs only.
- CCSP is a **vendor-neutral** certification of cloud security. CCSP aspirants can sit for the CCSP exam without passing CISSP beforehand.
- CSSLP focuses on software development security. The author treats it as an extension to the CISSP Domain 8. Individuals can go directly to CSSLP without receiving CISSP beforehand.
- PMI lays the management foundation for security professionals in terms of project management, business analysis, risk management, and strategy execution.
- IT Service Management (ITSM) helps to integrate security into IT processes and information systems.
- Software development is crucial to information security, as Agile approaches are commonly adopted nowadays, software solutions are deployed to the cloud, and security products rely on artificial intelligence (AI) for log correlation, intrusion detection, or other application.

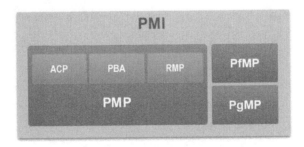

FIGURE 1-6 PMI CERTIFICATIONS

Security Governance

- Certified in the Governance of Enterprise IT (CGEIT) is about IT governance. It does not address security issues directly but is highly related to security in terms of IT and governance level.
- Certified Information Security Manager (CISM) addresses information security not only from the perspective of **management** but also from **governance**.
- Certified Information Systems Auditor (CISA) is ideal for internal auditors who work in the audit department as an **independent** organizational unit under the board-level **audit committee**.
- Certified in Risk and Information Systems Control (CRISC) focuses on information security risk management that is the foundation of CISA, CISM, and CGEIT.
- MBA/EMBA programs instill more business and governance agenda. A Ph.D. degree is helpful but optional.

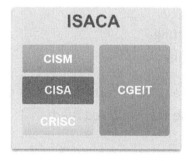

FIGURE 1-7 ISACA CERTIFICATIONS

Security Operations

Security operations are ongoing execution of repetitive security activities per the procedures to enforce security. The job market demands for certifications on security operations can be considered in terms of the **blue team** and the **red team**.

Blue Team

A blue team is a **defender** in a security exercise. It is "a group of individuals who perform an analysis of information systems to ensure security, identify security flaws, verify the effectiveness of each security measure, and to make certain all security measures will continue to be effective after implementation." (Wikipedia)

- Security Operations Center (SOC)
- Incident Response
- Intelligence Management
- Digital Forensics

Red Team

A red team is an **attacker** in a security exercise. It is "a group that helps organizations to improve themselves by providing opposition to the point of view of the organization that they are helping." (Wikipedia)

- Penetration Testing
- Social Engineering

EC-Council provides a suite of certifications to meet the market demands for the blue team and red team.

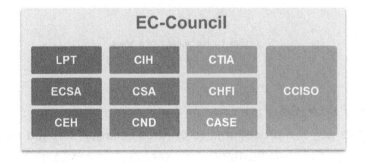

FIGURE 1-8 EC-COUNCIL CERTIFICATIONS

Infrastructure

Infrastructure refers to computer systems, networks, communication systems, operational systems, virtualization platforms, application runtimes, and the like.

The following diagrams demonstrate functional areas of the Infrastructure. There are a variety of certifications that map to each functional area. Cisco, Microsoft, RedHat, and VMWare are some of the most well-known certification providers.

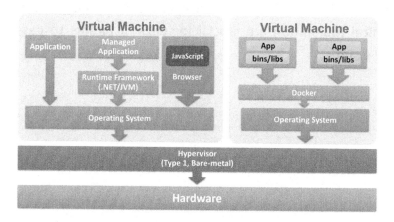

FIGURE 1-9 SAMPLE VIRTUALIZATION AND SOFTWARE PLATFORM

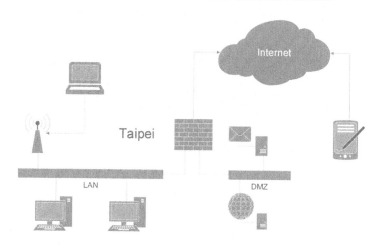

FIGURE 1-10 SAMPLE NETWORK INFRASTRUCTURE

1.2.4   CISSP's COMPREHENSIVE PERSPECTIVES

Information security is no longer limited to the technical domain but included in the business agenda. To support the business and the organization, CISSPs have to **think** from a variety of perspectives, such as board director, senior management, CISO, auditor, legal counsel, purchasing and HR staff, engineer, developer, project & program manager, end-user, attacker, and so forth.

Business mindset, **risk awareness**, and **solid management and technical foundation** are crucial for CISSP aspirants to pass the CISSP exam.

FIGURE 1-11 THE COMPREHENSIVE PERSPECTIVE OF CISSP

1.2.5   THE (ISC)² CBK

(ISC)² created and maintains the **Common Body of Knowledge (CBK)**, which defines global industry standards and best practices in information security, and aligns all certifications with the CBK.

The **CISSP CBK** is one of the CBKs on which the CISSP certification is developed. So do other certifications such as CISSP-ISSAP, CISSP-ISSEP, CISSP-ISSMP, CSSLP, CCSP, SSCP, CAP, and HCISPP.

A **body of knowledge (BOK)** is the complete set of concepts, terms, and activities that make up a professional domain, as defined by the relevant learned society or professional association.

The following are some well-known examples of BOK:

- The (ISC)² CBK, the Information Security sector
- The PMI PMBOK, the Project Management sector
- The IIBA BABOK, the Business Analysis sector

The CISSP CBK Reference/Guide

(ISC)² publishes official guides to the CBKs for each certification regularly - around every three years or so. The latest guide to the CISSP CBK is *The Official (ISC)² Guide to the CISSP CBK Reference, 5th Edition* (ISBN-10: 1119423341), published in 2019, also known as "The CBK." It is informative as a reference for CISSPs.

CISSP Study Guides

Most of the CISSP study guides available in the market are written based on the CISSP CBK as well. The *(ISC)² CISSP Certified Information Systems Security Professional Official Study Guide, 8th Edition* (ISBN-10: 1119475937) is the official (ISC)² study guide for the CISSP exam.

1.3   The CISSP Exam

1.3.1   CISSP and Information Systems

As CISSP stands for **"Certified Information Systems Security Professional,"** that is, you are pursuing being certified as a security professional of **"information systems,"** understanding the definition of an information system is decisive.

Definition

> An **information system** *is a system that converts data into information.*

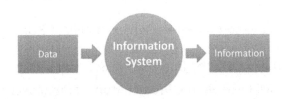

FIGURE 1-12 INFORMATION SYSTEM

- **Information** is useful data, or data with meaning, relevance, and purpose. This book uses data and information interchangeably unless otherwise stated.
- A **system** is a collection of related **elements** or **components** that work together to achieve a common purpose.

An **information system** typically comprises components such as 1) *data*, 2) *computer systems*, 3) *operating systems*, 4) *software*, 5) *networks*, 6) *data centers*, 7) *people*, 8) *business processes*, and so forth. This book introduced the **Peacock Model** as a metaphor for the information system.

An **information system** and its components are either **bought** or **made**. **Security engineering** addresses security concerns across the **system development life cycle (SDLC)**.

1.3.2   CISSP CERTIFICATION EXAM OUTLINE

The **CISSP Certification Exam Outline** (or "Exam Outline") is the compass in your CISSP journey. It guides your exam preparation direction and strategy.

Please download the **CISSP Certification Exam Outline** from the official (ISC)² web site before you get started your CISSP journey.

FIGURE 1-13 THE CISSP EXAM OUTLINE

Experience Requirements

CISSP candidates must have a minimum of 5 years of cumulative paid work experience in two or more of the eight domains. A candidate that doesn't have the required experience to become a CISSP may become an Associate of (ISC)² by successfully passing the CISSP examination.

Earning a 4-year college degree or regional equivalent or an additional credential from the (ISC)² approved list will satisfy one year of the required experience. Education credit will only satisfy one year of experience.

CISSP Domains

Think of the domains as topics you need to master based on your professional experience and education. The CISSP exam evaluates your expertise across **eight** security domains as follows.

1. Security and Risk Management
2. Asset Security
3. Security Architecture and Engineering
4. Communication and Network Security
5. Identity and Access Management (IAM)
6. Security Assessment and Testing
7. Security Operations
8. Software Development Security

This book broadly classifies them into **management** and **technical** domains weaved by Domain 1: Security and Risk Management.

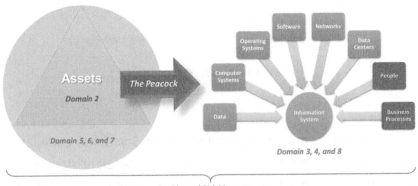

FIGURE 1-14 MANAGEMENT AND TECHNICAL DOMAINS

The eight CISSP domains can also be grouped into three disciplines:

- Security Governance
- Security Management (including security operations)
- Security Engineering

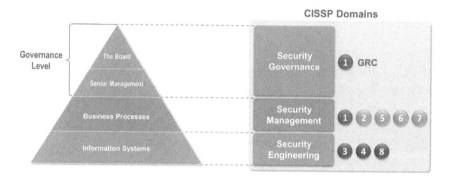

FIGURE 1-15 CISSP DOMAINS

Passing Standard

The passing standard is defined in terms of proficiency level:

- Below proficiency – below the passing standard
- Near proficiency – close to the passing standard
- **Above proficiency – above the passing standard**

CISSP candidates must score above the proficiency level **in all domains** to pass the CISSP exam. Even though (ISC)² does not publish the "passing score," to score over 70% in each domain is a reasonable expectation to be evaluated as "Above proficiency."

1.3.3 CISSP EXAM PREPARATION STRATEGY

There are four Critical Success Factors (CSFs) to pass the CISSP exam: conceptual model, comprehensive study, exam answering skills, and adequate work experience.

FIGURE 1-16 CISSP CRITICAL SUCCESS FACTORS

Conceptual Model

Firstly, stick to the **CISSP exam outline** and organize those topics into your **conceptual model**. CISSP exam preparation courses or boot camps may help build your conceptual model. The **Amicliens InfoSec Conceptual Model** is an example model for your reference.

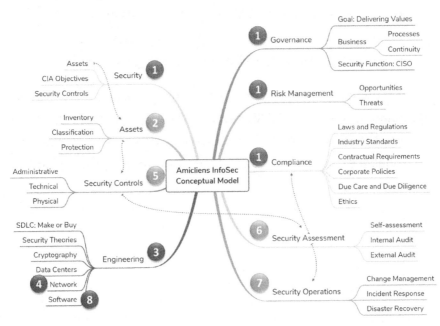

FIGURE 1-17 AMICLIENS INFOSEC CONCEPTUAL MODEL

Comprehensive Study

Secondly, study the **official (ISC)² study guide** or any book you prefer based on the **conceptual model** or the **CISSP exam outline** if you don't build one.

Refer to **NIST SP 800 series** guidelines and the **(ISC)² suggested references** as best as you can. It is an effective strategy to study CISSP domains with a **top/down** approach, in the sequence of **governance, management**, and **engineering**.

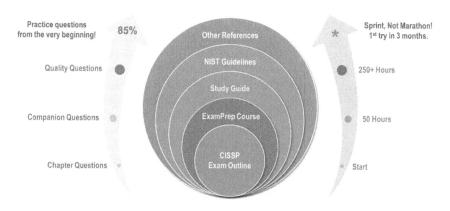

FIGURE 1-18 EXAM PREPARATION STRATEGY

Exam Answering Skills

Thirdly, **sharpen your exam answering skills** by practicing **quality questions** - your **reasoning process** and **justifications** for each answer option matter. Questions are not created equal - your reliance on creditable sources of quality questions matters.

There are three basic skills:

1. Reverse reading
2. Identifying sequence
3. Eliminating aliens

Browse the question in the **reverse order** to grasp the **main idea** of the question and to catch the **intuitive answer** at the first impression. Intuition triggers your powerful deep mind.

Answer options may be **sequential** but arranged in random order. Being aware of this arrangement and identifying the correct sequence helps answer the questions with "FIRST" or "MOST."

Eliminating aliens means ruling out those options that are apparently wrong. Select the survivor as your answer; don't rely on selecting the so-called "correct answer."

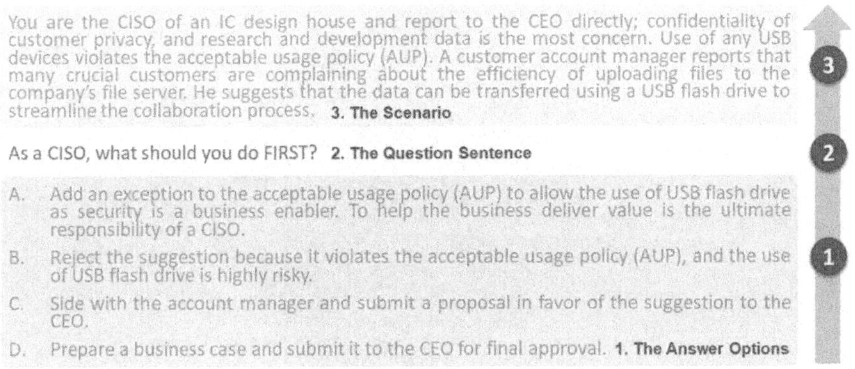

You are the CISO of an IC design house and report to the CEO directly; confidentiality of customer privacy, and research and development data is the most concern. Use of any USB devices violates the acceptable usage policy (AUP). A customer account manager reports that many crucial customers are complaining about the efficiency of uploading files to the company's file server. He suggests that the data can be transferred using a USB flash drive to streamline the collaboration process.   **3. The Scenario**

As a CISO, what should you do FIRST?   **2. The Question Sentence**

A.   Add an exception to the acceptable usage policy (AUP) to allow the use of USB flash drive as security is a business enabler. To help the business deliver value is the ultimate responsibility of a CISO.

B.   Reject the suggestion because it violates the acceptable usage policy (AUP), and the use of USB flash drive is highly risky.

C.   Side with the account manager and submit a proposal in favor of the suggestion to the CEO.

D.   Prepare a business case and submit it to the CEO for final approval. **1. The Answer Options**

FIGURE 1-19 REVERSE BROWSING

Adequate Work Experience

Last but not least, as most of the CISSP candidates do not have the work experience covering all the eight domains, **practicing questions** compensates **work experience**.

Do as many practice questions as you can. It is reasonable for CISSP aspirants to sit for the exam after completing at least 2000 questions. It is observed that non-native English speakers usually finished more than 5000 questions to pass the exam.

1.4 (ISC)² CODE OF ETHICS

Passing the CISSP exam is just part of the CISSP Certification program. You have to submit your endorsement application after provisionally passing the exam. The (ISC)² Board of Directors will award you the CISSP certification based on your exam results, application review, and acceptance of endorsement.

All (ISC)² members are required to commit to fully supporting the Code of Ethics, that has four canons:

I.   Protect society, the common good, necessary public trust and confidence, and the infrastructure.
II. Act honorably, honestly, justly, responsibly, and legally.
III. Provide diligent and competent service to principals.
IV. Advance and protect the profession.

Specificity of Complaints

The (ISC)² Ethics Committee is established by the Board of Directors to hear all ethics complaints and make recommendations to the board. The committee will consider only complaints that **specify** the canon of the (ISC)² Code of Ethics that has been violated.

Standing of Complainant

All complaints must be in writing, and they will be accepted only from those who claim to be **injured** by the alleged behavior.

Canon	Standing of Complainant
I or II	Any member of the public
III	Principals only (Those with an employer or contractor relationship with the certificate holder.)
IV	CISSPs or other certified professionals

TABLE 1-1 STANDING OF COMPLAINANT

REVIEW QUESTIONS

1. **Which of the following is not an (ISC)² certification?**
   A. HCISPP
   B. ISSEP
   C. CAP
   D. OSCP

2. **Which of the following is not a DoD 8570.1 baseline certification?**
   A. CISSP
   B. CISM
   C. CEH
   D. None of the above

3. **Which of the following is not a CISSP concentration certification?**
   A. ISSMP
   B. ISSAP
   C. ISSLP
   D. CSSLP

4. **Which of the following is the full spelling of CISSP?**
   A. Certified Information Systems Security Practitioner
   B. Certificate of Information Systems Security Professional
   C. Certification Information Systems Security Professional
   D. Certified Information Systems Security Professional

5. **Which of the following statement about the body of knowledge (BOK) is not true?**
   A. The complete set of concepts, terms, and activities
   B. A professional domain
   C. Defined by the relevant professional association
   D. Discrete and unstructured knowledge points

6. **Which of the following defines the scope of the CISSP exam?**

   A. The CISSP Certification Exam Outline

   B. The Ethics Complaint Affidavit Form

   C. The official (ISC)² Logo Usage Guidelines

   D. The (ISC)² CISSP Official Study Guide

7. **Which of the following is the primary CBK domain introduced in this book?**

   A. Security and Risk Management

   B. Security Assets

   C. Security Architecture and Engineering

   D. Identity and Access Management (IAM)

8. **According to the Peacock Model, which of the following is not an information system component?**

   A. Data

   B. Business processes

   C. Data centers

   D. Business strategies

9. **How many (ISC)² Code of Ethics Canons are there that are limited to principals only when making a complaint?**

   A. One canon

   B. Two canons

   C. Three canons

   D. Four canons

10. **Which of the following is not a critical success factor in passing the CISSP?**

    A. Build a conceptual model

    B. Study comprehensively

    C. Sharpen exam answering skills

    D. Use rote memory

2 SECURITY AND RISK MANAGEMENT

"Well, gentlemen, what is your business?"

- Peter Drucker

2.1 SECURITY

The main idea of **security** is about **protecting assets**. An asset is anything of **value** and worthy of **protection**. From the perspective of a Certified Information Systems Security Professional (CISSP), assets refer to the **information** and **information systems** (the **Peacock Model**).

In this book, security refers to **information security**, an umbrella term that covers **information systems security**, **information assurance**, and **cybersecurity**, unless otherwise stated.

2.1.1 WHAT IS INFORMATION SECURITY?

Definition

> *Information **Security** is a discipline of protecting **information** assets from **threats** through **safeguards** to achieve the **objectives** of confidentiality, integrity, and availability (Tier 3), or CIA for short, support business (Tier 2), and create and deliver values (Tier 1).*

Objectives and Risks

There are three tiers of **objectives**. Objectives in each tier are accompanied by **risks** that might affect their achievement.

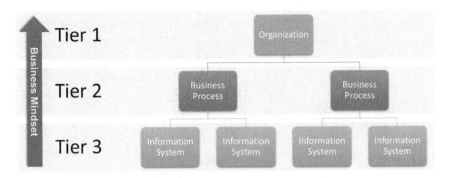

FIGURE 2-1 HIERARCHY OF OBJECTIVES

2.1.2   BUSINESS MINDSET

Information Security as Business Issues

Information security protects **information systems** from threats, streamlines **business processes** for efficiency and effectiveness, prevents them from disruption, and creates and delivers values at the **organization** level. As information security issues profoundly affect the business processes and organizational results, they should be treated not only as technical but as **business issues**.

Characteristics of Security Professionals

To solve information security issues, security professionals shall embody the **business mindset** and keep an eye on strategic goals, the supporting objectives, and related risks (opportunities and threats). Specifically, they won't treat Information security as a silo but align **information security objectives** with upstream **business and organizational goals**.

The following are critical characteristics of them:

- Think **strategically**.
- Focus on **values** and return on investment (ROI).
- Emphasize outcomes and **costs/benefits**.
- Execute **effectively** and efficiently.
- Innovate and enable **business**.
- Manage **performance** to improve continuously.
- Behave responsibly, ethically, and **legally**.

Management by Objectives (MBO)

Management is a systematic approach to achieve a goal or goals. Before managing anything, the **goals** or **objectives** must be set.

2.2 OBJECTIVES

2.2.1 INFORMATION SECURITY

Confidentiality, integrity, and **availability** (CIA) are the **objectives** of information security. On the other hand, disclosure, alteration, and disruption (DAD) compromise the security objectives.

FIGURE 2-2 CIA TRIAD AS SECURITY OBJECTIVES

The CIA triad as information security objectives is defined in Title III of the E-Government Act of 2002 (Public Law 107-347), also known as **FISMA**.

PUBLIC LAW 107–347—DEC. 17 2002   116 STAT. 2947

"§ 3542. Definitions

"(a) IN GENERAL.—Except as provided under subsection (b), the definitions under section 3502 shall apply to this subchapter.

"(b) ADDITIONAL DEFINITIONS.—As used in this subchapter:

"(1) The term 'information security' means protecting information and information systems from unauthorized access, use, disclosure, disruption, modification, or destruction in order to provide—

"(A) integrity, which means guarding against improper information modification or destruction, and includes ensuring information nonrepudiation and authenticity;

"(B) confidentiality, which means preserving authorized restrictions on access and disclosure, including means for protecting personal privacy and proprietary information; and

"(C) availability, which means ensuring timely and reliable access to and use of information.

FIGURE 2-3 FISMA

Confidentiality

"Preserving authorized restrictions on information access and disclosure, including means for protecting personal privacy and proprietary information..." [FISMA, 44 U.S.C., Sec. 3542]

A loss of *confidentiality* is the *unauthorized disclosure* of information. (FIPS 199)

Integrity

"Guarding against improper information modification or destruction, and includes ensuring information **non-repudiation** and **authenticity**..." [FISMA, 44 U.S.C., Sec. 3542]

A loss of *integrity* is the unauthorized *modification* or *destruction* of information. (FIPS 199)

Availability

"Ensuring timely and reliable access to and use of information..." [FISMA, 44 U.S.C., SEC. 3542]

A loss of *availability* is the disruption of access to or use of *information* or an *information system*. (FIPS 199)

FIGURE 2-4 SECURITY OBJECTIVES

More on Integrity

As defined in FISMA, 44 U.S.C., Sec. 3542, the "**Integrity**" objective also covers two well-known security properties: **authenticity** and **non-repudiation**. They are separated from "integrity" in the DoD Information Assurance (IA) program and the presidential cybersecurity policy.

Authenticity and non-repudiation, along with confidentiality, integrity, are vital objectives of cryptography. However, cryptography cannot achieve **availability**. Authentication message code (MAC) or digital signature can achieve authenticity. Digital signature can achieve non-repudiation.

Authenticity

Authenticity is "the property of being genuine and being able to be verified and trusted; confidence in the **validity of a transmission**, a **message**, or **message originator**." (NIST SP 800-53 Rev. 4)

Simply put, authenticity is the result of both **message verification** and **originator authentication** that render the confidence of the **message integrity** and **source validity**.

Non-repudiation

Non-repudiation is the "protection against an individual **falsely denying** having performed a particular action." (NIST SP 800-53 R4)

In a context of communication, the individual refers to either the sender or the recipient. Non-repudiation also refers to the "assurance that the **sender** of information is provided with proof of delivery and the **recipient** is provided with proof of the sender's identity, so neither can later deny having processed the information." (NIST SP 800-60 Vol. 1 R1)

2.2.2 INFORMATION ASSURANCE

Information Assurance (IA), a program of the US DoD per the Directive 8500.01E on October 24, 2002, extends the objectives of Information Security from the implicit three (CIA) to the explicit five that promote **authenticity** and **non-repudiation** as the first-class citizens.

FIGURE 2-5 INFORMATION ASSURANCE

The DoD Directive 8500.01E "establishes policy and assigns responsibilities under reference (a) to achieve Department of Defense (DoD) **information assurance (IA)** through a **defense-in-depth** approach that integrates the capabilities of **personnel**, **operations**, and **technology**, and supports the evolution to network centric warfare."

However, DoD Directive 8500.01 has transitioned to the term **cybersecurity**, which has replaced **"information assurance (IA)"** since **March 14, 2014**, to align with the Presidential Cybersecurity Policy, NSPD-54/HSPD-23.

Excerpt of DoD 8500.01

> *d. Adopts the term "**cybersecurity**" as it is defined in National Security Presidential Directive-54/Homeland Security Presidential Directive-23 (Reference (m)) to be used throughout DoD instead of the term "**information assurance (IA)**."*

2.2.3 CYBERSECURITY

Cybersecurity is defined in the Presidential Cybersecurity Policy, NSPD-54/HSPD-23, issued on **January 8, 2008**. The policy mandates the Comprehensive National Cybersecurity Initiative (CNCI) that outlines cybersecurity goals.

Excerpt of NSPD-54/HSPD-23

> *"**cybersecurity**" means prevention of damage to, protection of, and restoration of computers, electronic communications systems, electronic communication services, wire communication, and electronic communication, including information contained therein, to ensure its **availability**, **integrity**, authentication, **confidentiality**, and **non-repudiation**.*

However, the term **"authentication"** used in the **cybersecurity** policy does not align with the term **"authenticity"** defined in the **E-Government Act of 2002.**

NSPDs and HSPDs

The George W. Bush Administration started to issue National Security Presidential Directives (NSPDs) since February 13, 2001, to promulgate Presidential decisions on national security matters, and Homeland Security Presidential Directives (HSPDs) since October 29, 2001, for homeland security.

NSPDs and HSPDs are specific to the Bush Administration. The name of the documents is subject to change as the transition of the presidency. For example, the Trump Administration designated National Security Presidential Memoranda (NSPMs) to promulgate Presidential decisions on national security matters.

2.3 RISK

2.3.1 WHAT IS RISK?

Definition

According to ISO 31000, the **risk** is the **"effect of uncertainty on objectives."**

FIGURE 2-6 RISK FACTORS

Risk Factors

Uncertainty, objective, and effect are the most fundamental risk factors. The objective is the most crucial among the three.

- The **objective** can be established at relevant **functions** (such as financial, marketing, and information security) or different **tiers** (such as organization, business process, and information systems).
- **Uncertainty** unrelated to objectives will not shape a risk.
- The **effect** is a positive or negative deviation from what is expected. A **threat** is a risk with a **negative effect**, while an **opportunity** is a risk with a **positive effect**.

Risk factors are typically defined in the risk model to facilitate risk management. For example, risk must be linked to objectives when identifying risk; risk can be scaled in terms of risk factors when analyzing risk.

Traditionally, risk implies bad or negative things. Threats are intuitively related to risk because of the implication of loss, unsafe, or insecure. However, risk is a **neutral** term. The **concept of neutral risk** highlights the **business mindset**. Risk can be a **threat** and an **opportunity.**

FIGURE 2-7 THE CONCEPT OF NEUTRAL RISK

2.3.2   Security and Risk Management

It is the "**objective**" that glues and holds information security and risk management together. As a result, **Information security** can be viewed as a specialized discipline of **risk management** in terms of the effect of uncertainty on **hierarchical objectives**, as shown in **Figure 2-1 Hierarchy of Objectives**, across different tiers of the information system, business process, and organization.

2.3.3   Risk Glossary Matters

As terminologies may vary or be used inconsistently across risk management frameworks or methodologies, and risk happens in different **functions** and **tiers**, it is crucial to establish a shared **risk glossary** and concise **risk model** to communicate effectively.

A **risk model** facilitates risk management activities, such as risk identification, documentation, analysis, evaluation, and communication. The **NIST Generic Risk Model** and **Wentz's Risk Model** are specific risk models for information security.

2.4 WENTZ'S RISK MODEL

Wentz's Risk Model is based on **ISO 31000** and derived from the **NIST Generic Risk Model**. It comprises four members or member models:

1. The Simplified Generic Risk Model
2. The Peacock Model
3. The Onion Model
4. The Protection Ring Model

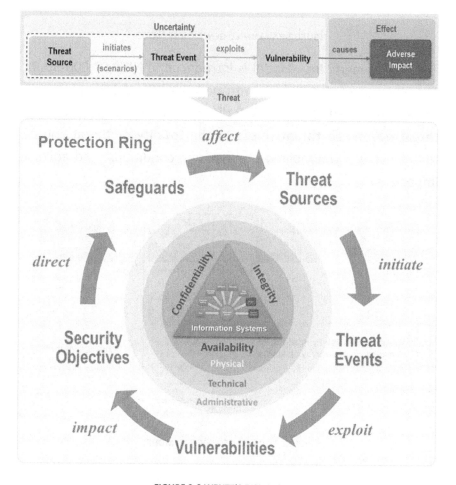

FIGURE 2-8 WENTZ'S RISK MODEL

2.4.1   THE SIMPLIFIED GENERIC RISK MODEL

This book simplified the **NIST Generic Risk Model** and elaborated risk factors in terms of **ISO 31000** (uncertainty and effect), that produced the **Simplified Generic Risk Model.**

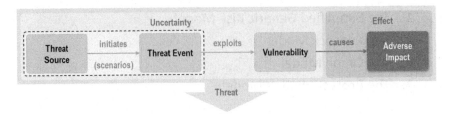

FIGURE 2-9 SIMPLIFIED GENERIC RISK MODEL

The NIST Generic Risk Model is introduced in NIST SP 800-30 R1. The concept of threat (risk with negative effects) in this model broadly aligns with ISO 31000. It distinguishes threat sources from threat events, so **threat** refers to the **totality** of threat source, threat event, vulnerability, predisposing conditions, and adverse impact.

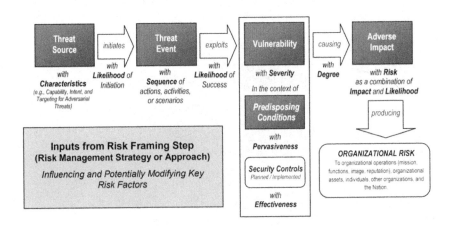

FIGURE 2-10 NIST GENERIC RISK MODEL

2.4.2   THE PEACOCK MODEL

Definitions

> An **information system** is a discrete set of information resources organized for the collection, processing, maintenance, use, sharing, dissemination, or disposition of information. In the context of this publication, the definition includes the **environment** in which the information system operates (i.e., **people, processes**, technologies, facilities, and cyberspace). (NIST SP 800-39)

The **Peacock Model** is a metaphor of **information systems** that extends the definition defined by **44 U.S.C, Sec 3502,** and aligns with this definition of NIST SP 800-39, as stated above.

This book treats **People** and **Business Processes** as extensions and part of an information system, as an information system is implemented and operated by people to support business processes.

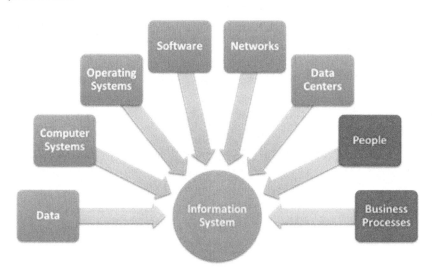

FIGURE 2-11 THE PEACOCK MODEL

Data and Information

As **Data** is converted into **information,** this book refers to them interchangeably unless otherwise mentioned.

To maintain data quality, 2.7.5 Data Governance has details.

People and Business Processes

Among those information system components, **People** are the most crucial assets. **Human life** must be protected at priority. People are also the weakest link in the information security chain.

End-users, system engineers, software developers, vendors, consultants, and contractors are familiar **stakeholders** of information systems, while administration, procurement, operation, marketing, sales, customer service, and information technology are typical **business processes.**

2.4.3 THE ONION MODEL

The **Onion Model** depicts the **layered defense** or **defense-in-depth** strategy. It implements a variety of categories of **safeguards** or **security controls** in **serial** and integrates **people, process, and technology (PPT)** or **personnel, operations, and technology (POT)** capabilities across the organization to enforce security.

Safeguards or security controls, as part of **risk treatment**, are implemented based on the result of **risk assessment** to protect information systems and achieve the security objectives of **confidentiality, integrity**, and **availability**.

Safeguards or security controls are typically categorized based on different schemes. **Administrative, technical (logical)**, and **physical** safeguards are specified in HIPAA.

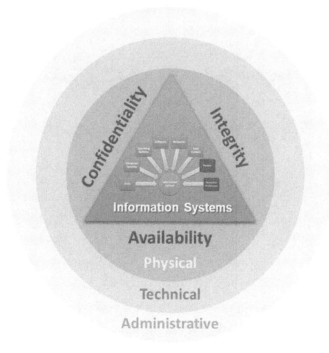

FIGURE 2-12 THE ONION MODEL

2.4.4   THE PROTECTION RING MODEL

The **Protection Ring Model**, in essence, is risk management at the level of information systems. It involves **risk assessment** (identification, analysis, and evaluation) and **risk treatment** processes to protect assets from **threats** through safeguards to achieve security objectives.

It is developed based on the **NIST Generic Risk Model** that distinguishes the **parts** (threat source, threat event, or impact) from the **whole** (threat).

This book treats a threat as a **holistic concept** that comprises threat source, threat event, and the adverse impact. It solves the communication problem that people tend to use the term "threat" without a sound definition.

FIGURE 2-13 THE PROTECTION RING MODEL

2.5 THREATS

2.5.1 WHAT IS A THREAT?

Definition

> A ***threat*** *is the negative effect of uncertainty on objectives. In the context of security, a threat is the adverse impact of potential on the security objectives*; the potential refers to the likelihood of **threat scenarios** *that one or more* **threat sources** *might initiate* a set of discrete **threat events** *to exploit* **vulnerabilities**.

The definition of threat above is based on **ISO 31000**, and the **NIST Generic Risk Model**. It is depicted as the following diagram:

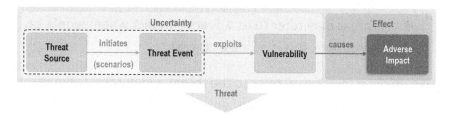

FIGURE 2-7 SIMPLIFIED GENERIC RISK MODEL

In this book, a **threat** is elaborated in terms of the three risk factors: objectives, uncertainty, and effect.

- The **objective** factor refers to security objectives, the CIA triad, cascaded with the upstreaming business and organizational goals.
- The **uncertainty** factor is the potential of **scenarios** that one or more **threat sources** may initiate a set of discrete **threat events** to exploit **vulnerabilities**.
- The **effect** factor is the adverse impact on the security objectives if the threat happens.

Inconsistent Definitions

- A **threat** is defined as "any **circumstance** or **event** with the potential to adversely impact organizational operations and assets..." and a **threat event** is defined as "an **event** or situation initiated or caused by a **threat source** that has the potential for causing adverse impact." (NIST SP 800-30)
- NIST SP 800-154 states, "the distinction between a **threat** and a **threat event** is subtle, but basically, a threat event is caused by a particular threat source, while a threat is more generic (not caused by a particular threat source)."
- According to the CISSP CBK Reference, 5th edition, a threat is an **actor** who potentially can compromise the operation of a system.
- A threat may refer to its **adverse impact** when people say, for example, this is a "huge" threat.

To sum up, a threat may refer to the threat event, threat source, or the adverse impact of a threat scenario.

Holistic Concept and Threat Statement

This book treats a threat as a **holistic concept** that comprises threat source, threat event, vulnerability, and the adverse impact. It's a good practice to use specific terms to remove vagueness and ambiguity when communicating in the context of risk.

The following threat or risk statement, using the risk metalanguage developed by Dr. David Hillson, is a good example that employs specific terms and demonstrates essential risk factors:

---

*Because a **hacker** (threat source) may deface an **unpatched web site** (vulnerability) through **SQL injection** (threat event), that would jeopardize the **organization's reputation** (adverse impact).*

2.5.2 THREAT SOURCE

A **threat source** is the cause of a threat. It is any party that may intentionally or accidentally initiate a **threat event** and also known as **threat agent** or **threat actor**. The following are common types of threat sources based on NIST SP 800-30 R1:

Adversarial

- Individual
- Group
- Organization
- Nation-State

Accidental

- User
- Privileged User/Administrator

Structural

- Information Technology (IT) Equipment
- Environmental Controls
- Software

Environmental

- Natural or man-made disaster
- Unusual Natural Event (e.g., sunspots)
- Infrastructure Failure/Outage

2.5.3   THREAT EVENT

A **threat event** is "an event or situation initiated or caused by a threat source that has the potential for causing adverse impact." It connects the **threat source** and **vulnerabilities**.

A threat event can be expressed in the format of **tactics, techniques,** and **procedures** (TTP). It's a good practice to describe a threat event by starting with a **verb** so that it can be matched with threat sources to shape **threat scenarios**.

The following are categories of threat events according to the NIST SP 800-30 R1:

- Perform reconnaissance and gather information
- Craft or create attack tools
- Deliver/insert/install malicious capabilities
- Exploit and compromise
- Conduct an attack (i.e., direct/coordinate attack activities)
- Achieve results (i.e., cause adverse impacts)
- Maintain a presence or set of capabilities
- Coordinate a campaign

The following table is an example of a threat event or TTP:

Threat Event	Perform perimeter network reconnaissance or scanning
Type	Perform reconnaissance and gather information
Description	The adversary uses commercial or free software to scan organizational perimeters to obtain a better understanding of the information technology infrastructure and improve the ability to launch successful attacks.

TABLE 2-1 TACTICS, TECHNIQUES, AND PROCEDURES (TTP)

2.5.4 THREAT SCENARIO

A **threat scenario**, a synonym for threat campaign, is "a set of discrete **threat events**, associated with a specific **threat source** or multiple **threat sources**, partially ordered in time." (NIST SP 800-30 R1)

Simply put, any combination between a **threat source** and a **threat event** forms a **threat scenario**. A complete threat scenario identifies not only the relationship between the threat source and threat events but also exploitable vulnerabilities by threat events. Other factors like **threat type** or **time** can also be taken into consideration for the complete description of a threat scenario.

FIGURE 2-14 THREAT SCENARIO

2.5.5 VULNERABILITY

Vulnerability is any "weakness in an information system, system security procedures, internal controls, or implementation that **could be exploited** or triggered by a **threat source**" (FIPS 200) through a **threat event** in a threat scenario. Safeguards or security controls reduce vulnerabilities and protect assets from threats.

2.5.6   ADVERSE IMPACT

The following examples of adverse impacts are an excerpt from NIST SP 800-30 R1.

Type of Impact	Impact
Harm to Operations	• Inability to perform current missions/business functions • Inability, or limited ability, to perform missions/business functions in the future • Harms due to noncompliance • Direct financial costs
Harm to Assets	• Damage to or loss of physical facilities • Damage to or loss of information systems or networks • Damage to or loss of information technology or equipment • Damage to or loss of component parts or supplies • Damage to or of loss of information assets • Loss of intellectual property
Harm to Individuals	• Injury or loss of life • Physical or psychological mistreatment • Identity theft • Loss of Personally Identifiable Information • Damage to image or reputation
Harm to Other Organizations	• Harms due to noncompliance • Direct financial costs
Harm to the Nation	• Damage to or incapacitation of a critical infrastructure sector • Loss of government continuity of operations • Damage to current or future ability to achieve national objectives

TABLE 2-2 EXAMPLES OF ADVERSE IMPACTS

2.5.7 THREAT MODELING

Definition

> In systems and software engineering, threat modeling is a "systematic exploration technique to expose any circumstance or event having the potential to cause harm to a system in the form of destruction, disclosure, modification of data, or denial of service." It results in a vulnerability assessment. (ISO 24765:2017)

Common Forms of Threat Modeling

NIST SP 800-154 defines threat modeling as a form of risk assessment that models' aspects of the attack and defense sides of a particular logical entity (software, system, or data).

It introduces two primary forms of threat modeling: **software threat modeling** and **system threat modeling**, while **data-centric system threat modeling** is a particular type of system threat modeling.

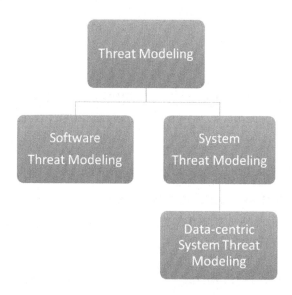

FIGURE 2-15 COMMON FORMS OF THREAT MODELING

Attack Vector

In threat modeling, a threat scenario can be expressed as an **attack vector**, which is "a segment of the entire pathway that an attack uses to access a vulnerability." (NIST SP 800-154)

In mathematics and physics, a vector a quantity with both magnitude and direction. "Specifically, an attack vector is a means by which a threat agent can abuse of weaknesses or vulnerabilities on assets (including human) to achieve a specific outcome." (ENISA, 2018)

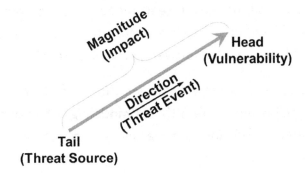

FIGURE 2-16 ATTACK VECTOR

Attack Surface

Attack surfaces of information systems are "**exposed areas** that make those systems more vulnerable to cyber attacks." (NIST SP 800-53 R4)

The exposed areas are **accessible areas**, typically the interfacing points of **input and output**, where weaknesses or deficiencies in information systems that provide opportunities for adversaries to exploit vulnerabilities.

In short, the **attack surface** is the sum of the identified attack vectors.

Attack surface review

Attack surface reviews or threat modeling ensure that developers analyze both design and implementation changes to information systems and mitigate attack vectors; for example, deprecation of unsafe functions.

Microsoft Threat Modeling

There are a variety of threat modeling approaches, such as OCTAVE, PASTA, VAST, Trike, and so forth. Microsoft threat modeling is one of the most popular approaches.

There are five major threat modeling steps:

1. Define security requirements.
2. Create an application diagram.
3. Identify threats.
4. Mitigate threats.
5. Validate that threats have been mitigated.

Threat modeling should be part of your routine development lifecycle, enabling you to refine your threat model and further reduce risk progressively.

It uses STRIDE to categorize threats and DREAD to analyze, score, and prioritize them.

STRIDE	DREAD
• Spoofing	• Damage
• Tampering	• Reproducibility
• Repudiation	• Exploitability
• Information Disclosure	• Affected users
• Denial of Service	• Discoverability
• Elevation of Privilege	

TABLE 2-3 STRIDE AND DREAD

2.5.8   THREAT LANDSCAPE

Definition

A threat landscape is a collection of threats in a particular domain or context, with information on identified vulnerable assets, threats, risks, threat actors and observed trends. (ENISA, 2015)

The European Union Agency for Cybersecurity (ENISA) publishes a report called the "ENISA Threat Landscape Report" each year since 2012. The ENISA threat landscape (ETL) is a collection of threats collected from publicly available information (open-source intelligence or OSINT), one source of **threat intelligence**.

The ETL report provides an overview of threats and an independent view on observed **threats**, **threat agents**, and **threat trends**. It also consists of a list with **top threats** prioritized according to the frequency of appearance and NOT according to the impact caused.

Threat Intelligence

"Threat intelligence is evidence-based knowledge, including context, mechanisms, indicators, implications and action-oriented advice about an existing or emerging menace or hazard to assets. This intelligence can be used to inform decisions regarding the subject's response to that menace or hazard." (Gartner, 2013)

Threat intelligence can be collected from, but not limited to, the following sources:

- Publicly available information (open source)
- Social media
- People
- The deep and dark web (DDW)

2.6 Safeguards

Safeguards are protective measures against threats, also known as **countermeasures, security controls,** or **controls** for short. These terms are often used interchangeably. However, please note that the ISACA CISM exam distinguishes controls (the means) from countermeasures (the process).

Safeguard Taxonomy

Safeguards or **security controls** are typically classified based on different schemes, and it leads to a variety of terms, e.g., types, categories, families, or classes.

For example, the following terms are commonly used:

- HIPAA groups security controls into three **categories**
- (ISC)² CISSP CBK proposes seven **types**
- NIST SP 800-53 R4 groups into 18 **families**
- ISO 27001 Annex A has 14 primary **categories**

A security control can be classified into different or more than one control category in terms of its **control objective**, nature, property, or any other criteria.

Control Objectives

Control objectives direct the planning, implementation, and evaluation of security controls. They provide specific targets for auditors to evaluate the effectiveness of security controls. Besides, they can be classified so that risk practitioners can identify risks, for example, compliance, financial reporting, strategic, or operations.

2.6.1   HIPAA SAFEGUARDS

According to the Health Insurance Portability and Accountability Act of 1996 (**HIPAA**), it defines three categories of safeguard: **administrative, physical,** and **technical,** as shown in the following clause:

---

(2) Safeguards

Each person described in section 1320d-1(a) of this title who maintains or transmits health information shall maintain reasonable and appropriate administrative, technical, and physical safeguards-

    (A) to ensure the integrity and confidentiality of the information;

    (B) to protect against any reasonably anticipated-

        (i) threats or hazards to the security or integrity of the information; and

        (ii) unauthorized uses or disclosures of the information; and

    (C) otherwise to ensure compliance with this part by the officers and employees of such person.

CMS Regulations: The Privacy and Security Rule

The Centers for Medicare & Medicaid Services (CMS) issues regulations, known as the **Privacy Rule** and **Security Rule**, to define and specify safeguards applicable to those entities covered by HIPAA. The Privacy Rule, primarily, addresses how **Protected Health Information (PHI)** can be used and disclosed, while the Security Rule, as a subset of the Privacy Rule, applies specifically to **Electronic Protected Health Information (ePHI).**

Administrative Safeguards

The Security Rule defines administrative safeguards as, "administrative actions, and policies and procedures, to manage the selection, development, implementation, and maintenance of **security measures** to protect electronic protected health information and to manage the conduct of the covered entity's **workforce** in relation to the protection of that information." The critical point of administrative safeguards is: they manage "**security measures**" and "**the conduct of workforce.**"

Administrative safeguard is roughly equivalent to **management (NIST) or directive (ISC2) control**. Some study guides don't explicitly define "administrative" controls; they name some examples and relate administrative controls to policies, procedures, and something like that. It conflicts with the definition in the Security Rule in some way as both technical and physical safeguards include "policy and procedures" according to the Security Rule.

Technical Safeguards

The Security Rule defines technical safeguards as "the **technology** and the policy and procedures for its use that protect electronic protected health **information** and control **access** to it."

Technical safeguard is also known as **logical control** compared with the physical controls. The key point of technical safeguards is: they protect **"information"** through access control.

Physical Safeguards

The Security Rule defines physical safeguards as "physical **measures**, policies, and procedures to protect a covered entity's electronic information **systems** and **related buildings and equipment**, from natural and environmental hazards, and unauthorized intrusion."

The key point of physical safeguards is: they protect **"systems"** and **"related buildings and equipment"** from "hazards" and "intrusion."

However, it is not uncommon for people to treat all policies and procedures are administrative controls.

2.6.2   SECURITY CONTROL FRAMEWORKS

A **security control framework** is a collection of **security controls** and **implementation and audit guidelines** well-organized as a template or solution for organizations to mitigate risks.

NIST Special Publications 800-53 R4 and ISO 27001 are two of the most well-known security control frameworks. NIST publications are applicable to the US government agencies, while ISO 27001 applies to almost all organizations. Taiwan government tends to implement information security management systems (ISMS) compliant with ISO 27001.

Scoping and Tailoring

An organization can **select** security controls from a security control framework and **customize** it based on organizational requirements as a **security baseline**. The selection and customization processes are also known as **scoping** and **tailoring**.

Risk Management

Risks at information systems level are handled by embedding security controls across the assets life cycle and the systems development life cycle (SDLC). The baseline security controls are then implemented, assessed, and monitored as part of the risk management - risk response.

The following are some well-known risk management frameworks:

ISO	NIST
• ISO 31000 • ISO 27005	• NIST SP 800-30 R1 • NIST SP 800-37 R2 • NIST SP 800-39

TABLE 2-4 ISO AND NIST RISK STANDARDS AND GUIDELINES

NIST Special Publications 800-53 R4

The following catalog of controls comes from NIST SP 800-53 R4, while the assessment objectives are defined in NIST SP 800-53A R4.

ID	FAMILY
AC	Access Control
AT	Awareness and Training
AU	Audit and Accountability
CA	Security Assessment and Authorization
CM	Configuration Management
CP	Contingency Planning
IA	Identification and Authentication
IR	Incident Response
MA	Maintenance
MP	Media Protection
PE	Physical and Environmental Protection
PL	Planning
PS	Personnel Security
RA	Risk Assessment
SA	System and Services Acquisition
SC	System and Communications Protection
SI	System and Information Integrity
PM	Program Management

TABLE 2-5 NIST CONTROL FAMILIES

It provides the initial control baselines in determining security controls for information systems based on the impact level. The number, AC-2 (1), refers to the first **control enhancement** to AC-2. AC-2 (1) is "AUTOMATED SYSTEM ACCOUNT MANAGEMENT."

CNTL NO.	Control Name	Priority	Initial Control Baselines		
			LOW	MOD	HIGH
Access Control					
AC-2	Account Management	P1	AC-2	AC-2 (1) (2) (3) (4)	AC-2 (1) (2) (3) (4) (5) (11) (12) (13)

TABLE 2-6 EXCERPT OF CONTROL BASELINES FROM NIST SP 800-53 R4

ISO 27001 Annex A

The following table is a summary from the ISO 27001 Annex A that is directly derived from and aligned with those listed in ISO/IEC 27002:2013, Clauses 5 to 18.

ID	Category
A.5	Information security policies
A.6	Organization of information security
A.7	Human resource security
A.8	Asset Management
A.9	Access control
A.10	Cryptography
A.11	Physical and environmental security
A.12	Operations security
A.13	Communications security
A.14	System acquisition, development and maintenance
A.15	Supplier relationships
A.16	Information security incident management
A.17	Information security aspects of business continuity management
A.18	Compliance

TABLE 2-7 ISO CONTROL CATEGORIES

A control category is divided into subcategories. Each subcategory is associated with a control objective, which is supported by a couple of controls. For example,

A.5 Information security policies		
A.5.1 Management direction for information security		
Objective: To provide management direction and support for information security in accordance with business requirements and relevant laws and regulations		
A.5.1.1	Policies for information security	*Control* A set of policies for information security shall be defined, approved by management, published and communicated to employees and relevant external parties.

TABLE 2-8 CONTROL OBJECTIVE AND CONTROLS

2.6.3   (ISC)² ACCESS CONTROL TYPES

According to (ISC)², there are seven **access control** types. This book organizes them based on the timing of unauthorized behaviors driven by the factors of **motive, opportunity**, and **means** (MOM).

Before	During	After	Others
1. Directive	4. Detective	6. Recovery	7. Compensating
2. Deterrent	5. Corrective		
3. Preventive			

TABLE 2-9 (ISC)² ACCESS CONTROLS

1. **Directive controls** promote security **awareness** and direct compliant **behaviors**, e.g., policies, posters, and signs.

2. **Deterrent controls** discourage violation of security policies and reduce or eliminate the **motive** of unauthorized behaviors, e.g., guards and mantraps.

3. **Preventive controls** raise the hurdle and thwart the breaching attempts, e.g., firewalls, intrusion prevention systems (IPS), and antivirus software.

4. **Detective controls** monitor and report potential or undergoing breaching attempts, e.g., intrusion detection systems (IDS), honeypots or honeynets, and reviews.

5. **Corrective controls** stop the breaching attempts to maintain or restore normal operations or service levels, e.g., Trusted Recovery and Antivirus Software (Quarantining a virus).

6. **Recovery controls** recover from disruption and restore operations to normal service level if the attempts of breaching have disrupted the operations or services, e.g., backup, system imaging, and shadowing.

7. **Compensating controls** provide **contingent** or **alternative** protection to existing controls. For example, a PIN code is compensating for the Windows Hello facial recognition.

2.6.4 ACCESS CONTROL MECHANISMS

Definitions

- **Identity** is "an attribute or set of attributes that uniquely describe a subject within a given context." (NIST SP 800-63-3)
- **Attribute** is "a quality or characteristic ascribed to someone or something." (NIST SP 800-63-3)
- **Subject** is to "an active entity, generally in the form of a person, process, or device, that causes information to flow among objects or changes the system state." (NIST SP 800-33)
- **Object** is "a passive entity that contains or receives information." (NIST SP 800-33)
- **Access** is a subject's behavior "to obtain the use of a resource." (ISO/IEC 20944-1:2013)
- **Label** is "the means used to associate a set of security attributes with a specific information object as part of the data structure for that object." (NIST SP 800-53 R4)
- **Clearance** is "a formal security determination by an authorized adjudicative office that an individual is authorized access, on a need to know basis, to a specific level of classified information (TOP SECRET, SECRET, or CONFIDENTIAL)." (CNSSI 4005)

Identity Management

Enrollment is the process of registering a **subject** in a **directory** and binding the **secrecy** (or **authenticator**) to its identity after **identity proofing** (if necessary).

When creating or provisioning a new account, it is crucial to focus on proofing the applicant's identity. That is, the identity shall be **unique,** and its attributes shall be **authentic**, **genuine**, and

accurate. The applicant shall be linked to a real-life subject. Identity proofing is the primary concern of Identity Assurance Levels (IAL).

Entitlement is the process of granting **privileges** (permissions and rights), also known as **authorization**.

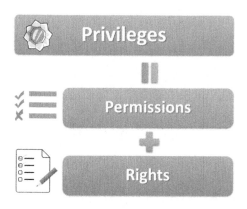

FIGURE 2-17 PRIVILEGES

Both enrollment and entitlement are parts of **identity provisioning**, which is the process of creating user accounts and granting privileges across systems in a streamlined or automatic way. It helps streamline identity and access management processes across the user life cycle.

In other words, the provisioning process relies on automation, technologies, and tools. As Gartner stated,

- Provisioning tools use approaches such as cloning, roles, and business rules so that businesses can automate onboarding, offboarding and other administration workforce processes (for example, new hires, transfers, promotions, and terminations).
- Provisioning tools also automatically aggregate and correlate identity data from HR, CRM, email systems, and other "identity stores." (Gartner, 2020)

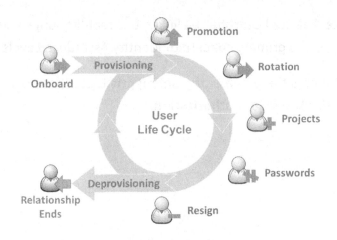

FIGURE 2-18 USER LIFE CYCLE

User Provisioning Example

Imagine that you're preparing a user account for a new employee.

- HR system: a detailed employee record
- PACS (physical access control system)
- Enterprise portal
- ERP systems
- Cloud services
- VDI (Virtual Desktop Infrastructure)

You may have to create a couple of user accounts and credentials (keycards, smartphone, or biometric) and grant privileges across those systems mentioned above.

It is error-prone and takes much time to do it manually. Moreover, the employee may be promoted, rotated, fired, or resign. The privileges granted have to be updated.

This is when provisioning comes in. It addresses the cumbersome process of creating and updating accounts and privileges through automation.

Access Control Methods

Access is typically managed or controlled by three methods: **authentication, authorization, and accounting (AAA)**.

- **Authentication** is the process of "verifying the identity of a user, process, or device, often as a prerequisite to allowing access to resources in an information system." (FIPS 200) **Identification** is the process of a subject claiming, or professing, an identity so that the authentication process can proceed.
- **Authorization** is "the process of verifying that a requested action or service is approved for a specific entity." (NIST SP 800-152)
- **Accounting** is the process of recording entries or logs of the activities of subjects and objects, just like keeping financial accounting journals.

Accounting, Auditing, and Accountability (Yet Another AAA)

Logs are the work product of accounting; the **audit trail** refers to a set of correlated logs. **Auditing** is the process of reviewing or examining logs. **Accountability** can be achieved through auditing the audit trail to trace the activity to an entity uniquely.

- **Accountability** is "the security objective that generates the requirement for actions of an entity to be traced uniquely to that entity." (NIST SP 800-33)
- **Audit** is the "independent review and examination of records and activities to assess the adequacy of system controls, to ensure compliance with established policies and operational procedures." (NIST SP 800-12 Rev. 1)
- **Audit trail** is "a chronological record that reconstructs and examines the sequence of activities surrounding or leading

to a specific operation, procedure, or event in a security-relevant transaction from inception to final result." (NIST SP 800-53 Rev. 4)

This book treats accounting and auditing in **the opposite way** to the Sybex Official CISSP Study Guide. It defines **auditing** as "recording a log of the events and activities related to the system and subjects," and **accounting** (aka accountability) as "reviewing log files to check for compliance and violations in order to hold subjects accountable for their actions."

Reference Monitor: The Origin of Access Control

The concept of access control was first known as the **reference monitor concept**, which is introduced in the Anderson Report by James P. Anderson & Co. in October of 1972.

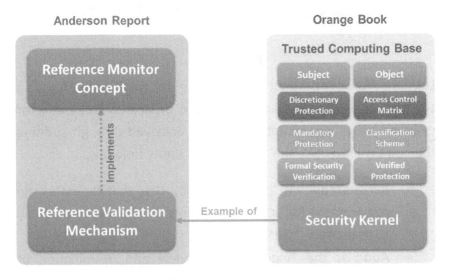

FIGURE 2-19 REFERENCE MONITOR CONCEPT

Security Kernel

In a trusted computing system, the security mechanisms or capabilities are collectively called a **trusted computing base (TCB)**. The **security kernel**, part of the TCB, is the implementation of the reference monitor and in charge of **access control** (authentication, authorization, and accounting).

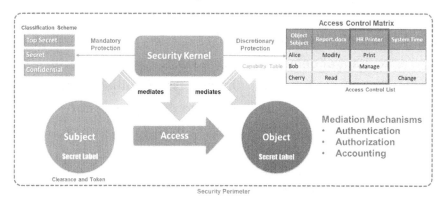

FIGURE 2-20 SECURITY KERNEL

The following diagram is a simplified example that depicts the access control process from the perspective of users:

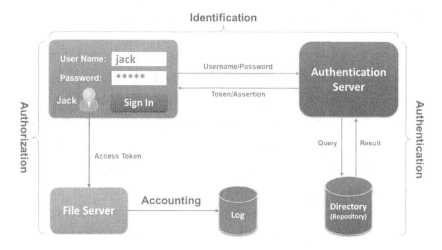

FIGURE 2-21 IDENTIFICATION + AAA

1. **Identification** is the process that Jack shows (claims or professes) his identity to the authentication server.
2. The **authentication server** verifies the identity against the directory and returns a token or asserts his claims if the identity is genuine.
3. Jack reads from or writes to the **file server** by submitting the access token. The file server makes authorization decisions based on authorization policies, e.g., access control matrix, sensitivity labels, roles, rules, or attributes, to grant or deny the access request.
4. The events happen in the process of authentication, and authorization will be recorded to the **log repository**.
5. A **session** refers to the period from Jack's signing to the system to his sign-out.

2.6.5 SECURITY POSTURE

Security posture is "the **security status** of an enterprise's networks, information, and systems based on information assurance resources (e.g., people, hardware, software, policies) and capabilities in place to manage the defense of the enterprise and to react as the situation changes." (NIST SP 800-30 R1)

In other words, **security posture** is the overall security status of an organization determined by the effectiveness of total security controls established throughout the life cycle of assets. For example, an organization takes inventory of assets, classifies them based on business values, selects controls from security control frameworks, customizes security controls according to business requirements as the security baseline. The baseline security controls are then implemented for certification, assessed for authorization, and monitored for assurance. Changes are managed, and actions are taken to improve continuously.

2.7 ASSETS

Definition

> An **asset** is anything that has **value** to an organization. *(ISO 22300:2018)*

An asset's value can be determined based on certain evaluation criteria, such as original cost, market value, potential income, replacement or re-creation cost, or costs incurred due to the loss of security objectives. Asset value is one of the most crucial **asset classification** factors.

The more valuable an asset is, the higher the degree of protection. However, **Cost/benefit** is one of the most fundamental risk management principles. Protection mechanisms typically cover assets worthy of protection only. In other words, if the cost of mitigating risk is **higher than** the asset value, the risk will not be handled or accepted.

2.7.1 ASSET TYPES

Assets can be tangible or intangible. The standard of ISO 27005 divides assets into **primary assets** and **supporting assets.**

Type	Asset
Primary Assets	• Information • Business processes and activities
Supporting Assets	• Hardware • Software • Network • Site • Personnel • Organization's structure

TABLE 2-10 ASSET TYPES

2.7.2   ASSET INVENTORY

An **inventory** keeps records of assets.

ISO 27001 requires:

- **Assets** associated with information and information processing facilities shall be identified and an inventory of these assets shall be drawn up and maintained.
- **Rules** for the acceptable use of information and assets associated with information and information processing facilities shall be identified, documented and implemented.
- All **employees** and external party users shall return all of the organizational assets in their possession upon termination of their employment, contract or agreement.

Configuration Management Database (CMDB)

The **configuration management database (CMDB)** is a well-established IT asset inventory that stores information on all the significant entities, such as hardware, software, documents, business services, and also the people assets.

Those entities are referred to as **Configuration Items (CI)**. Changes to the CMDB shall follow the process of **Configuration Management**.

However, the CMDB is not a general-purpose asset repository. It is designed to support the IT environment where the interrelations between the CIs are maintained.

2.7.3 ASSET OWNERSHIP

Once an asset is located and identified, an **asset owner** shall be assigned. Asset owners are **accountable** for the assets they are assigned ownership in terms of security, privacy, and intellectual property rights.

There are different types of **asset owners**, as an organization delivers products or services by performing business processes supported by one or more information systems that process a variety of types of data.

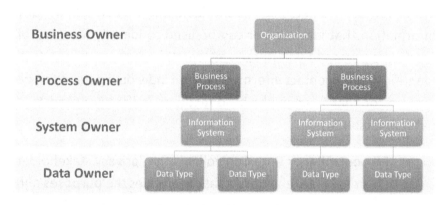

FIGURE 2-22 ASSET OWNERS

The **system owner** shall coordinate with **data owners** to determine the security controls needed based on the information types and the system's **impact level**. To learn more about how to select controls based on the result of system categorization, please refer to the NIST SP 800-53 R4 for details.

Personal Data

However, **personal data** are not created or owned by the organization that collects and controls them; instead, the ownership belongs to the **data principal** or **data subject**. A data subject is a natural person to whom the personal data refer.

GDPR defines **personal data** as "any information relating to an identified or identifiable natural person ('data subject'); an identifiable natural person is one who can be identified, directly or indirectly, in particular by reference to an identifier such as a name, an identification number, location data, an online identifier or to one or more factors specific to the physical, physiological, genetic, mental, economic, cultural or social identity of that natural person."

Personally identifiable information (PII)

ISO 29100 defines Personally identifiable information (PII) as "any information **that** identifies or can be used to identify, contact, or locate the person to whom such information pertains, from which identification or contact information of an individual person can be derived, or **that** is or might be directly or indirectly linked to a natural person."

- **PII Controller** or Data Controller is the "privacy stakeholder (or privacy stakeholders) that determines the **purposes** and **means** for processing personally identifiable information (PII) other than natural persons who use data for personal purposes." (ISO 29100)
- **PII Processor** or Data Processor is the "privacy stakeholder that processes personally identifiable information (PII) **on behalf of** and **in accordance with** the **instructions** of a PII controller." (ISO 29100)

Protected health information (PHI)

ISO/TS 14441:2013 defines protected health information (PHI) as "information about an identifiable person that relates to the physical or mental health of the individual, or to provision of health services to the individual."

In a broad sense, it may include any part of a patient's medical record or payment history.

Privacy

Privacy is "the right of a party to maintain control over and confidentiality of information about itself." (NISTIR 4734)

A **privacy policy** is a statement or a legal document (in privacy law) that discloses some or all of the ways a party gathers, uses, discloses, and manages a customer or client's data. It fulfills a legal requirement to protect a customer or client's privacy.

Privacy Principles

The following are ISO 29100 privacy principles:

1. Consent and choice
2. Purpose legitimacy and specification
3. Collection limitation
4. Data minimization
5. Use, retention and disclosure limitation
6. Accuracy and quality
7. Openness, transparency, and notice
8. Individual participation and access
9. Accountability
10. Information security
11. Privacy compliance

2.7.4   ASSET CLASSIFICATION

Asset classification is the process of a systematic arrangement of assets by assigning an asset to a **named class** (group, category, tier, or level) based on **criteria** such as legal or regulatory requirements, sensitivity, criticality, impact, or business value to determine its **protection requirements**. A **classification scheme** refers to the named classes, criteria, and procedures used for classification.

Security labels or labels (e.g., Secret) defined in the classification scheme can be used to enforce **mandatory access control (MAC)**. Classified assets in the MAC environment are protected through security labels in the internal operations of systems. To get access to the classified information, a person must have a **security clearance** at an appropriate level and a need-to-know.

Security Marking

The term security marking refers to "the association of security attributes with **objects** in a human-readable form, to enable organizational **process-based** enforcement of information security policies." (NIST SP 800-53 R4)

Classified assets should be appropriately marked according to the marking guideline to enforce security, e.g., photographs, films, recordings, slides, charts, graphs, folders, CDs, documents, etc.

Security Labeling

The term security labeling refers to "the association of security attributes with **subjects** and **objects** represented by internal data structures within organizational information systems, to enable information **system-based** enforcement of information security policies." (NIST SP 800-53 R4)

Classification by Sensitivity

Sensitivity is "a measure of the importance assigned to information by its owner, for the purpose of denoting its need for protection." (NIST SP 800-60 Vol. 1 R1) However, the importance is typically measured in terms of the degree of impact to the security objective of **confidentiality** resulting from loss or unauthorized access to sensitive data.

It is common to classify data based on its sensitivity. For example, the following **military-based** classification scheme based on sensitivity is a regulatory requirement, or a mandate of Executive Order 13926 specifically. The **business** classification scheme is more flexible that can be crafted according to the organization's requirements.

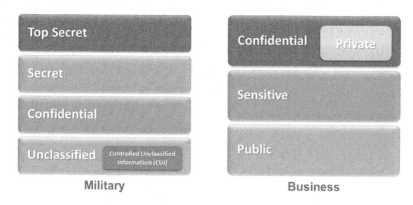

Military   Business

FIGURE 2-23 CLASSIFICATION SCHEME

Classification by Criticality

Criticality is "a measure of the degree to which an organization depends on the information or information system for the success of a mission or of a business function." (NIST SP 800-60 Vol. 1 R1) Criticality is typically evaluated in terms of the security objective of **availability**.

For example, when conducting business impact analysis (BIA), the criticality of a business process is determined by the maximum tolerable downtime (MTD). Business processes with higher criticality (shorter MTD) are restored at priority.

Classification by Impact

The impact is the negative effects on objectives. When it comes to information security, the impact on security objectives can be evaluated in terms of the CIA triad, confidentiality, integrity, and availability. It is common to evaluate the impact of an information system based on the types of **information** it processes. A high-impact system needs more protection than a low-impact system.

FIPS 199 defines the procedure to evaluate the overall impact level of an information system based on the information types. "**Categorize System**" is the first step defined in the **NIST SP 800-37 R2**, Risk Management Framework for Information Systems and Organizations - A System Life Cycle Approach for Security and Privacy.

FIGURE 2-24 RISK MANAGEMENT FRAMEWORK

Example of System Categorization

For example, a **SCADA system** handles two types of information: **sensor data** and **administrative information.**

Information Type	Confidentiality	Integrity	Availability
Sensor Data	NA	HIGH	HIGH
Administrative Information	LOW	LOW	LOW
High-water Mark	**LOW**	HIGH	HIGH

The high-water mark for the **individual** impact level of **confidentiality** is LOW, **integrity** is HIGH, and **availability** is HIGH.

The impact level of Integrity or availability, HIGH, is the high-water mark, so the **overall** information system impact level is HIGH. The **SCADA system** is a **HIGH-impact system.**

Please refer to FIPS 199 & NIST SP 800-60 Vol. 1 and 2 and FIPS 200 & NIST SP 800-53 R4 for details.

Classification by Business Value

Value is anything of importance, significance, use, or benefit. Business value expands the concept of value beyond economic value to include other forms of value, many of which are not directly measured in monetary worth.

In terms of information security, the business value may include considerations of **asset value, sensitivity, criticality, impact level, legal or regulatory requirements**, and so forth.

Sample Classification Scheme

The city of Washington, D.C., implemented a new data policy in 2017 to be more transparent while remaining secure.

Please refer to the following URL for details:
https://octo.dc.gov/page/district-columbia-data-policy

Level	Usage	Protection Needs
Level 4	Restricted Confidential	• Disclosure, transmission, or dissemination of Level 4 data to other agencies within the District shall not occur unless it is approved in advance.
Level 3	Confidential	• Data shall be secured via encryption, whether the data are at rest or in transit, and by additional safeguards such as digital certificates for integrity and non-repudiation. • It may be accessed and used by internal District parties only when specifically authorized to do so in the performance of their duties. • External parties requesting this information for authorized public body business must be under a contractual obligation of confidentiality with the public body before receiving it. • Information identified as Level 3 or above shall not be accessible to the public in any way.
Level 2	For District Government Use	• Data shall not be posted on the public Internet or exposed to search engines. • It will, however, be made available upon request directly to the requesting entity.
Level 1	Public Data	• Not Proactively Released. • Data not protected from public disclosure or subject to withholding under any law, regulation, or contract. • Publication of the data on the public Internet would have the potential to jeopardize the safety, privacy, or security of anyone identified in the information.
Level 0	Open Data	• Data readily available to the public on open government websites and datasets.

TABLE 2-11 EXAMPLE CLASSIFICATION OF WASHINGTON, D.C.

2.7.5 DATA GOVERNANCE

As information is the organization's primary asset and data quality can be a legal or regulatory requirement in some sectors, data governance becomes trending, but without an agreed definition. As a result, this book defines data governance as follows:

Definition

> *Data governance is the responsibility of the board and executive management to ensure data fits its purpose and compliant with applicable legal and regulatory requirements through the practice of overall enterprise data management (EDM).*

Data governance emphasizes the top-down approach that the governance level is aware of the strategic role of data, committed to, and accountable for enterprise data management.

The purpose of enterprise data management is to consolidate data from different sources, unify data semantics and rules, improve data quality and decision-making, discover business opportunities, and support strategic goals.

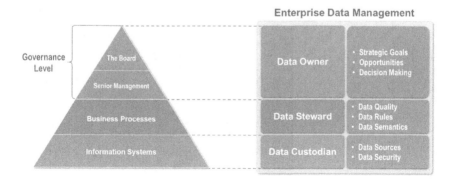

FIGURE 2-25 DATA GOVERNANCE

Data Governance Roles

There are three typical roles in a data governance program: data owner, data steward, and data custodian.

Data Role	Responsibilities
Owner	✓ Senior management ✓ Accountable for the data ✓ Data classification ✓ Authorization
Steward	✓ Data semantics and rules ✓ Data quality
Custodian	✓ Day-to-day security administration ✓ Backup and restore

TABLE 2-12 DATA ROLES

Data Architecture

Data architecture is a crucial part of the enterprise data management, which is supported, from the perspective of technology, by metadata management, data dictionary, data quality, data analysis, impact analysis, data integration, monitoring and reporting, master data management, and so forth.

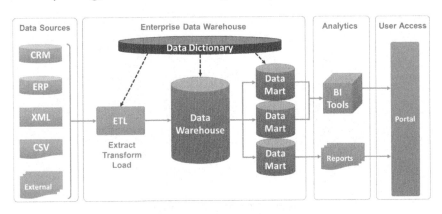

FIGURE 2-26 DATA ARCHITECTURE

Metadata is "data that provides information about other data." In short, it's data about data.

Schema is one type of metadata, which formally defines the name, type, attributes, constraints, relationship, structure, etc. of data.

The **data dictionary** is, in essence, a metadata repository that standardizes the definition of a data element and enables a consistent interpretation of data elements.

Data Life Cycle

Data is the encoded fact with a life cycle and finite states. Encoding is the recording process of facts in a specific expression format. Data exist in the state of at rest, in motion, or in use; they typically go through the life cycle of being created or collected, stored, used, shared, archived, and destroyed.

The data life cycle and data states help in designing and implementing security controls. For example, collecting personal data that should meet privacy principles or applicable regulations is a typical concern in the "Create" stage.

FIGURE 2-27 DATA LIFE CYCLE

E-Discovery

Information governance also plays a crucial role in E-Discovery. Electronic discovery or "e-discovery" refers to discovery of information stored in electronic format (often referred to as Electronically Stored Information, or ESI).

Discovery is the pre-trial phase in a lawsuit in which each party investigates the facts of a case, through the rules of civil procedure, by obtaining evidence from the opposing party and others by means of discovery devices including requests for answers to interrogatories, requests for production of documents and things, requests for admissions, and depositions.

- Requests for answers to interrogatories
- Requests for production of documents and things
- Requests for admissions
- Depositions

The Electronic Discovery Reference Model (EDRM) is a conceptual view of the stages in the e-discovery process. It is iterative, not a literal or waterfall model.

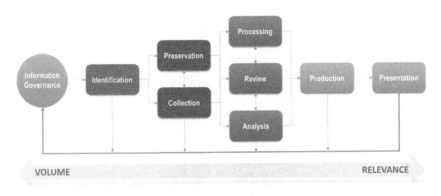

FIGURE 2-28 ELECTRONIC DISCOVERY REFERENCE MODEL

2.7.6 SYSTEM ENGINEERING

Information systems are either **made** in-house or **bought** from external entities. To build or purchase a **secure** information system or any of its components falls in the discipline of **Systems Security Engineering**, or **Security Engineering** for short.

- **Systems Engineering** is a discipline of applying knowledge to create or acquire a system that is composed of interrelated elements collaborating for a common purpose throughout the system development life cycle (SDLC), or system life cycle (SLC). A life cycle is a collection of predefined stages and processes. "Development" here implies construction or procurement.

- **Security Engineering** is a specialty discipline of systems engineering. It addresses the protection needs or security requirements throughout the system life cycle.

Security engineering is introduced in Domain 3 that covers the system life cycle, foundational security concepts and theories, cryptography, and related thematic topics, such as sites and facilities (Domain 3), network and communication (Domain 4), and software development (Domain 8).

Engineering Standards

The following are some of the most well-known organizations or standards bodies that proposed system engineering standards or methodologies:

- EIA: Electronic Industries Alliance, ceased in 2011
- IEEE: The Institute of Electrical and Electronics Engineers
- ANSI: American National Standards Institute
- IEC: International Electrotechnical Commission

- ISO: International Organization for Standardization
- NIST: National Institute of Standards and Technology
- INCOSE: International Council on Systems Engineering

NIST and ISO are crucial to the CISSP exam. NIST SP 800-160 V1 addresses **systems security engineering** based on ISO 15288. It superseded NIST SP 800-64 R2 that addresses security considerations in the **system development life cycle (SDLC)**. Even though superseded, NIST SP 800-64 R2 is still worth reading.

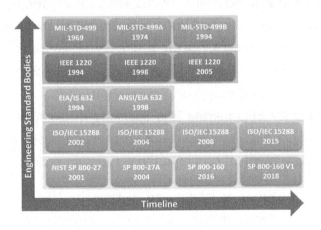

FIGURE 2-29 SYSTEM ENGINEERING STANDARDS

ISO 15288 System Life Cycle

The **life cycle** is the finite set of generic phases and steps a system may go through over its entire life history. (ISO 15704:2000)

FIGURE 2-30 ISO 15288 SYSTEM LIFE CYCLE

ISO 15288 Life Cycle Processes

Process Groups	Processes
Agreement Processes	1. Acquisition 2. Supply
Organizational Project-Enabling Processes	1. Life Cycle Model Management 2. Infrastructure Management 3. Portfolio Management 4. Human Resource Management 5. Quality Management 6. Knowledge Management
Technical Management Processes	1. Project Planning 2. Project Assessment and Control 3. Decision Management 4. Risk Management 5. Configuration Management 6. Information Management 7. Measurement 8. Quality Assurance
Technical Processes	1. Business or Mission Analysis 2. Stakeholder Needs and Requirements Definition 3. System Requirements Definition 4. Architecture Definition 5. Design Definition 6. System Analysis 7. Implementation 8. Integration 9. Verification 10. Transition 11. Validation 12. Operation 13. Maintenance 14. Disposal

TABLE 2-13 ISO 15288 LIFE CYCLE PROCESSES

NIST SDLC Phases and Security Activities

NIST has aligned Systems Security Engineering (NIST SP 800-160 v1) and Risk Management Framework (NIST SP 800-37 R2) with ISO 15288 and obsoleted the legacy System Development Life Cycle (NIST SP 800-64 R2).

NIST SP 800-64 R2 introduced a 5-phase model of SDLC as follows:

SDLC Phases	Major Security Activities
Initiation	1. Initiate Security Planning 2. Categorize the Information System 3. Assess Business Impact 4. Assess Privacy Impact 5. Ensure Use of Secure Information System Development Processes
Development/Acquisition	1. Assess Risk to System 2. Select and Document Security Controls 3. Design Security Architecture 4. Engineer in Security and Develop Controls 5. Develop Security Documentation 6. Conduct Testing (Developmental, Functional and Security)
Implementation/Assessment	1. Create a Detailed Plan for C&A 2. Integrate Security into Established Environments or Systems 3. Assess System Security 4. Authorize the Information System
Operations/Maintenance	1. Review Operational Readiness 2. Perform Configuration Management and Control 3. Conduct Continuous Monitoring
Disposal	1. Build and Execute a Disposal/Transition Plan 2. Ensure Information Preservation 3. Sanitize Media 4. Dispose of Hardware and Software 5. Closure of System

TABLE 2-14 SECURITY ACTIVITIES ACROSS SDLC

2.8 MANAGEMENT

Definition

Management *is a systematic approach to achieve a goal or goals.*

FIGURE 2-31 MANAGEMENT

What is a Goal?

A **goal** is a written statement of **desired outcomes** or **future state**. **Success** is the result of achieving the goal.

Systematic Approach

The **PDCA** cycle an iterative four-step approach: Plan, Do, Check, and Act. It is one of the most commonly adopted approaches and adopted as the core concept of ISO standards.

- Plan: set the objectives of the system and processes to deliver results ("What to do" and "how to do it")
- Do: implement and control what was planned
- Check: monitor and measure processes and results against policies, objectives and requirements and report results
- Act: take actions to improve the performance of processes

2.8.1 GOALS

Definition

> A **goal** is a written statement of **desired outcomes** or **future state**.

A well-developed goal meets the **SMART** criteria as follows:

- Specific - a specific goal can be described with a statement of success supported by CSFs, critical success factors.
- Measurable - a measurable goal can be divided into a set of objectives defined by metrics and KPIs, key performance indicators.
- Achievable - an achievable goal should be with reasonable targets regarding metrics or KPIs.
- Realistic - a realistic goal takes resources and constraints into considerations.
- Timely - a timely goal has a deadline.

Goals and Objectives

According to ISO 22301, **objective** means the "**result to be achieved**." It is not uncommon to use words with similar meanings interchangeably, such as **aim**, **goal**, or **target**, or to express an objective in another way, e.g., **intended outcome**, **purpose**, **operational criterion**. "Goals" and "Objectives" are often used interchangeably. However, in this book, goals may imply some differences as the following table shows:

Goals	Objectives
• Broad	• Specific
• Long-term	• Short-term
• Upper-level	• Lower-level
• Measured by KGIs (or KPIs)	• Measured by KPIs

TABLE 2-15 GOALS AND OBJECTIVES

Hierarchy of Objectives

A goal is typically broken down into objectives that are then broken down further to a reasonable level **hierarchically**. The hierarchy is **not** limited to two levels. It is common to organize objectives into three levels: **strategic, tactical,** and **operational.**

FIGURE 2-32 HIERARCHY OF OBJECTIVES

KGI and KPI

A goal is an **upper-level** objective (parent) relative to the **lower-level** ones (children) broken down from it, given a hierarchy of objectives. A goal is measured by Key Goal Indicators (KGIs), while its subsidiary objectives are measured by Key Performance Indicators (KPIs). KGI is a measure for the outcome, while KPI is a measure for performance. A KGI at the lower level serves as a KPI to the parent KGI.

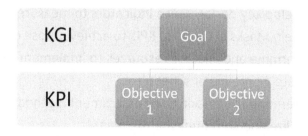

FIGURE 2-33 GOALS AND OBJECTIVES

2.8.2 PLAN

The purpose of the "Plan" step is to set the **objectives** and **processes** to deliver results. ("What to do" and "how to do it")

Objective Setting

An objective can be broken down into one or more tasks or work, which is converted into results by a process.

- A **task** is 1) a specific piece of work to be done, 2) a set of actions intended to accomplish a set of functions, or 3) an activity or activities required to achieve an intended outcome, objective, or goal.
- A **process** is a "set of interrelated or interacting activities which transforms inputs into outputs."

Planning Process

The purpose of the planning process is to achieve the objectives and intended outcomes. **Plans** are the output of the planning process. Typically, there are different types of plans in terms of the goal they aim to achieve. For example, strategic plans, tactical plans, operating plans, and project plans.

The following are generic planning process:

1. Breaking down upstream goals to develop objectives
2. Develop key performance indicators to measure success
3. Develop tasks in terms of KPIs to achieve those objectives
4. Determine and allocate resources to implement tasks
5. Create a timeline or schedule
6. Determine the tracking and assessment method
7. Finalize and communicate the plan

2.8.3 Do

The purpose of the "Do" step is to implement and control what was planned. At this stage, objectives, tasks, processes, budgets, schedules, and resources are determined.

Execution is about leading **people** to complete **tasks** under **budget** and within the **schedule** to produce **quality** output while keeping **stakeholders** informed and supportive.

Effectiveness and Efficiency

Effective execution leads to success – the achievement of objectives or goals. The **effectiveness** of performance refers to the production contributes or related to objectives, while **efficiency** is the measure of employing fewer resources to create more output. The output of a task will be **verified** internally for the **correctness** and **validated** externally for **effectiveness**.

Transition to Check and Act

Executing processes will produce **performance data**, which will be collected and fed into controlling processes to generate **performance information** and **performance report** that will then be communicated to stakeholders.

Based on the performance report, **corrective actions** that shall follow the **change management** process will be taken for **continuous improvement**.

2.8.4 CHECK

The purpose of the "Check" step is to 1) monitor and measure processes and results against policies, objectives, and requirements, and 2) report results.

Performance Measurement

The terms "goal" and "objective" are often used interchangeably. However, there are some differences. A goal is a written statement of desired outcomes or future state; an objective is the result to be achieved. A goal is typically broken down into objectives.

Performance is a measurable result used to measure the progress to the objective or goal. **Success** is the result of achieving a goal.

FIGURE 2-34 PERFORMANCE MEASUREMENT

KGI and KPI

A goal is an upper-level objective (parent) relative to the lower-level ones (children) broken down from it, given a hierarchy of objectives. A goal is measured by Key Goal Indicators (KGIs), while its subsidiary objectives are measured by Key Performance Indicators (KPIs). KGI is a measure for the outcome (the effect), while KPI is a measure for performance (the cause). A KGI at the lower level serves as a KPI to the parent KGI.

The term KGI comes from COBIT, which distinguishes KGI as a lagging indicator from KPI as a leading indicator. A **leading** indicator measures the progress toward an objective; a **lagging** indicator determines if a goal is achieved. However, it's not uncommon to call a KGI just KPI.

Measure

A **measure** is a variable with "a standard unit used to express the size, amount, or degree of something" (Google Dictionary).

For example, if you stand up on a scale to measure weight, you will get a measurement, say 85KG. In this case, **weight** is the measure, **85** the quantity, and **KG** the unit used.

In other words, a **measure** collects facts, but it isn't associated with an objective or goal, while a metric does.

The following are common categories of measures:

Scale of Measure	Example
Nominal	Male, Female
Ordinal	Very Bad, Bad, Fair, Good, Very Good
Internal	Temperature with the Celsius scale
Ratio	The Kelvin temperature scale

TABLE 2-16 CATEGORIES OF MEASURES

Measurement is a process to determine a value; it also refers to the result of a measurement.

Measurements are values of a variable, or instances of a measure.

Metric and Indicator

A **metric** is a quantitative measure that is associated with an objective or goal so that the performance can be measured.

An **indicator** is also a measure, but it can be either **quantitative** or **qualitative**.

For example, if your **objective** is to lose weight 30KG (from 100KG to 70KG) in one year, "weight loss" is the **metric** to manage your progress to the objective. After six months of effort, you reached 85KG.

That means you have lost the weight of 15KG (KPI) or achieved 50% of the goal (KGI). Your performance is **GOOD**. On the contrary, if you lost weight **3KG** only after six months, the small quantity of **3KG** (quantitatively) indicates your performance is **POOR** (qualitatively).

FIGURE 2-35 KPI AND KGI

Key Risk Indicator (KRI)

Risk is the effect of uncertainty on objectives. A KPI measures the progress to the objective, while a Key Risk Indicator (KRI) measures the deviation to the objective.

Specifically, a KRI is an indicator that indicates the level of risk an activity carries or measures the likely deviation to your objective or goal. Putting KRI widgets on a dashboard is an excellent idea to manage risk visually.

For example, extreme weight might danger people's health. When the weight is less than 40KG or higher than 100KG, it will danger health. If you decide to maintain health by controlling the weight at around 70KG, weight is the KRI that measures the likely deviation to your objective.

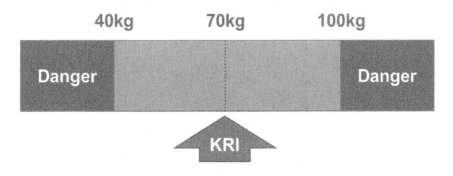

FIGURE 2-36 WEIGHT AS A KRI FOR HEALTH MANAGEMENT

2.8.5 ACT

The purpose of the "Act" step is to take action to improve the performance of processes.

Problem Solving Process

Risk becomes an **issue** when it materializes, that affects performance or progress to objectives. If an issue is solved with temporary handling or **workaround** without identifying the **root cause**, it may reoccur and become a problem. A **problem** can only be remedied with a solution that has identified the **root cause**.

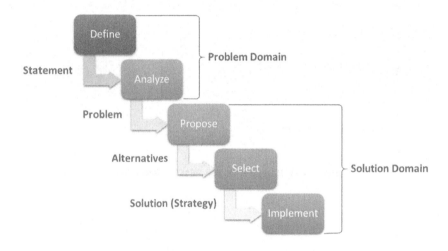

FIGURE 2-37 PROBLEM SOLVING PROCESS

Root Cause Analysis (RCA)

In science and engineering, root cause analysis (RCA) is a method of problem solving used for identifying the root causes of faults or problems. RCA generally serves as input to a remediation process whereby corrective actions are taken to prevent the problem from reoccurring. There are a variety of RCA techniques, such as Fish-Bone Diagram or Ishikawa Diagram, 5-Whys Analysis, Pareto Analysis, Fault Tree Analysis, and so forth.

Corrective Actions

Once the root cause is identified, corrective actions that shall follow the change management process will be taken for continuous improvement.

- **Corrective action** is action to eliminate the cause(s) of a nonconformity (non-fulfillment of a requirement) and to prevent a recurrence.
- **Continuous improvement**, or **continual improvement**, is a recurring activity to enhance performance.

Change Management

Even if we have worked out a solution, we cannot apply the solution at our discretion as corrective actions almost always cause changes to baselines. For example, the **scope**, **budget**, **schedule**, **performance measurement**, **security controls**, or **configurations** are well-established baselines.

Change management is the process of protecting **baselines** from **creeping** or unauthorized changes.

Baselines

Baselines are anything of importance that requires signoff or approval to control changes against them. Baselines may be subject to change due to **corrective actions** or **continuous improvement** resulting from **performance review** or **problem-solving process**.

A security control baseline is the minimum requirement of security that is typically determined by the security control scoping and tailoring process. A snapshot of configurations can serve as a security baseline.

REVIEW QUESTIONS

1. **Which of the following mandates the security objectives of confidentiality, integrity, and availability?**
   A. GDPR
   B. FISMA
   C. GLBA
   D. SOX

2. **Which of the following is not a risk constituent factor according to ISO 31000?**
   A. Objectives
   B. Uncertainty
   C. Effect
   D. Appetite

3. **Which of the following is not part of Wentz's Risk Model?**
   A. Peacock
   B. Onion
   C. Protection Ring
   D. State Machine

4. **Because a hacker may deface an unpatched web site through SQL injection, that would jeopardize the organization's reputation. Which of the following best describes the statement?**
   A. Threat
   B. Threat event
   C. Threat source
   D. Attack Surface

5. **According to ISO 27005, which of the following is not a primary asset?**
   A. Financial reports
   B. End users

C. Procurement processes

D. Customer profiles

6. **Which of the following data classification criteria covers the most widespread concerns?**

   A. Sensitivity

   B. Criticality

   C. Business value

   D. Recovery cost

7. **Which of the following is responsible for improving data quality?**

   A. Data owner

   B. Data custodian

   C. Data controller

   D. Data steward

8. **Which of the following best describes security labeling?**

   A. Stick a "Secret" label to a CD

   B. Use a red document folder with the term "Secret"

   C. Configure a printer as "Secret"

   D. Place security level "(S)" inline in a text

9. **Which of the following is not part of access control?**

   A. Authentication

   B. Authorization

   C. Accounting

   D. Availability

10. **Which of the following is the most critical element of management?**

    A. Goals or objectives

    B. Planning

    C. Execution

    D. Continuous improvement

3 GOVERNANCE, RISK, AND COMPLIANCE

"The bottom line is determined by those at the top."

- Ljupka Cvetanova, The New Land

3.1   GRC AS A DISCIPLINE

Definition

> GRC is the integrated collection of capabilities that enable an organization to reliably achieve objectives, address uncertainty and act with integrity. (OCEG, 2019)

GRC refers to **Governance**, **Risk Management**, and **Compliance**. The first research on GRC was published by Scott L Mitchell in 2007. He serves as the chairman and CEO of a nonprofit think tank called the Open Compliance and Ethics Group (OCEG).

OCEG was founded in 2002, facing the "dot com bust" and notable corporate failures such as Enron (2001), Worldcom (2002), and Healthsouth (2002). Its initial mission was to improve corporate compliance and ethics.

This book treats GRC as an integrated discipline and risk management and compliance as crucial issues of governance.

FIGURE 3-1 GRC AS A DISCIPLINE

3.2   WENTZ'S GOVERNANCE MODEL

Wentz's Governance Model, as the following diagram shows, is a generic governance model that integrates the concept of GRC, the philosophy of governance for values, and a general strategic management process.

Sound governance achieves the ultimate goals of creating and delivering values and fulfilling organizational missions with the constraints of resources and taking into account risk and compliance.

Strategic management is the core of governance. Strategies are formulated and executed within the context of the organization that can be described by the enterprise architecture. Business areas, organizational structure, processes, and technologies are primary dimensions of the enterprise architecture.

FIGURE 3-2 WENTZ'S GOVERNANCE MODEL

3.3   GOVERNANCE FOR VALUES

3.3.1   WHAT IS GOVERNANCE?

Definition

> **Governance** is the **overall practices** exercised by the board of directors and senior management (the **governance level**) who directs and controls the **organization**, allocates and optimizes the **resources**, and holds the **ultimate responsibility** for the outcomes to create and deliver **values** and achieve organizational **missions**.

IT Governance Institute

The IT Governance Institute defines governance as the set of responsibilities and practices exercised by those responsible for an organization (e.g., the board of directors and executive management in a corporation, the head of a federal agency) with the express goal of:

- providing strategic direction,
- ensuring that organizational mission and business objectives are achieved,
- ascertaining that risks are managed appropriately, and
- verifying that the organization's resources are used responsibly.

The Governance Level

According to the Cambridge Dictionary, governance is "the way that organizations or countries are managed at the highest level and the systems for doing this."

The highest level in an enterprise typically refers to the board of directors and senior management (also known as the executive or top management), collectively called the governance level. It governs the enterprise to realize its mission and vision and achieve its goals and undertakes accountability for the results.

FIGURE 3-3 THE GOVERNANCE LEVEL

Organization Types

An **organization** is an entity with an organized group of people conducting business (enterprise), social (non-governmental or non-profit), political (government), and other activities for a common purpose.

A **company** is an organization conducting business activities for profits, e.g., manufacturing, trading, or service. A **corporation**, as an enterprise, is a legal business entity, typically controlled and directed by the board of directors. This book uses the **company**, **business**, and **enterprise** interchangeably unless otherwise stated.

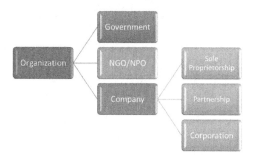

FIGURE 3-4 ORGANIZATION TYPES

3.3.2   STRATEGIC MANAGEMENT

The purpose of governance is to create and deliver values and fulfill organizational missions with the constraints of resources and taking into account risk and compliance.

Strategic management is the core of governance. Strategies are formulated and executed within the context of the organization that can be described by the enterprise architecture. Business areas, organizational structure, processes, and technologies are primary dimensions of the enterprise architecture.

General strategic management process can be described as follows:

1. Craft the mission statement and communicate the vision
2. Define strategic goals and measurable objectives
3. Develop and align strategies that comprise initiatives
4. Allocate and optimize resources to maximize values
5. Measure and monitor performance to achieve objectives
6. Manage risks to respond to changes and ensure success
7. Behave responsibly to maintain integrity and compliance

They can be mapped into the following diagram:

FIGURE 3-5 GOVERNANCE FOR VALUES

3.3.3 ENTERPRISE ARCHITECTURE

Definition

> **Enterprise architecture** (EA) is a conceptual blueprint that defines the **structure** and **operation** of an organization. (TechTarget, 2007)

- **Enterprise** is one or more organizations sharing a definite mission, goals, and objectives to offer an output such as a product or service. (ISO, 2000)
- **Architecture** is a description (model) of the basic arrangement and connectivity of parts of a system (either a physical or a conceptual object or entity). (ISO, 2000)
- **Structure** is the definition of the relationships among the components of an organization. (ISO, 2000)
- **Operation** is the collaboration of organizational components through consuming organizational resources and conducting organizational processes and activities to create and deliver values.

In essence, enterprise architecture is a **structural abstraction** of an enterprise from various **perspectives** to manage **complexity**, e.g.,

- Business: products, services, and organization's capabilities
- Structure: organizational units, people, and roles
- Processes: value chains and information and material flow
- Technologies: infrastructure, systems, and data

A well-structured organization can be examined from the perspectives of the **static** organizational structure and **dynamic** organizational processes and the **holistic** view of enterprise architecture.

Benefits of Enterprise Architecture

As the purpose of governance is to direct and control the organization and create and deliver values, it is crucial to understand how the business operates, and how the underlying information systems and technologies support the operations in a secure environment to help achieve business success.

However, information security is a business issue. It not only protects information and information systems but also supports business and organizational objectives.

It is where Enterprise Architecture comes into play because Enterprise architecture as a management practice provides an integrated view that engages business and technical people working together to solve business problems.

It's an effective way for security professionals to comprehend the organizational structure, processes, and infrastructure and manage protection needs and security requirements through enterprise architecture.

To sum up, Enterprise Architecture provides the following benefits:

- Providing insights into the organization and its operations
- Reducing IT investment wastes
- Bridging business and technologies
- Facilitating communication
- Guiding system design and development
- Addressing potential single points of failure
- Supporting systems security engineering

Enterprise Architecture Frameworks

An enterprise architecture framework provides principles and practices for creating and using the architectural description (text, diagrams, or models) of an enterprise. Zachman (1987), TOGAF (1995), and the Federal Enterprise Architecture Framework (1999) are well-known enterprise architecture frameworks.

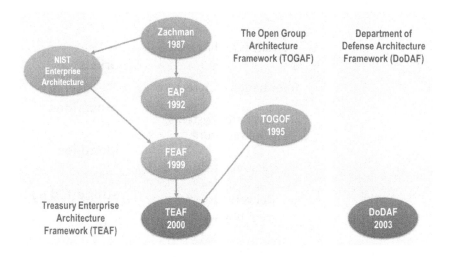

FIGURE 3-6 ENTERPRISE ARCHITECTURE FRAMEWORKS

Zachman

The study of enterprise architecture first emerged in 1987 with the article in the IBM Systems Journal, "A Framework for Information Systems Architecture," by J.A. Zachman. It was then renamed "The Zachman Framework for Enterprise Architecture." The Zachman Framework is **NOT** a methodology for constructing an enterprise architecture but a taxonomy for organizing architectural artifacts.

TOGAF

The Open Group Architecture Framework (TOGAF) is developed starting in 1995 by The Open Group. It introduces comprehensive architectures, e.g., business, applications, data, and technical architecture.

NIST Enterprise Architecture

The NIST Enterprise Architecture Model, initiated in 1989, is obsolete.

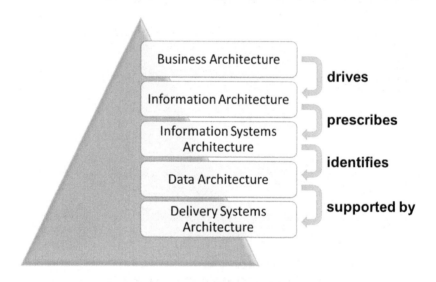

FIGURE 3-7 NIST ENTERPRISE ARCHITECTURE MODEL INITIATED IN 1989

FEAF

The Federal Enterprise Architecture Framework (FEAF) defines a collection of interrelated reference models, including Performance, Business, Service Component, Data, and Technical as well as more detailed segment and solution architectures.

Enterprise Security Architecture

It is worth noting that the Enterprise Security Architecture (ESA) is a part of enterprise architecture (EA) focusing on information security throughout the enterprise. Sherwood Applied Business Security Architecture (SABSA) is one of the most well-known ESAs.

3.3.4   ORGANIZATIONAL STRUCTURE

A typical organizational structure comprises three levels: first-line staff, middle management, and the governance level. The governance level refers to the **board of directors** and **senior management** (C-suite/Top/Executive management).

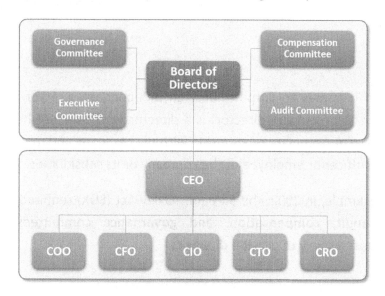

FIGURE 3-8 GOVERNANCE STRUCTURE

The Board of Directors

A board is "a group of people constituted as the decision-making body of an organization." (Google Dictionary)

The board of directors, or the board for short, is a group of directors, who are elected by a corporation's shareholders or organization's members to:

1. Represent and advance shareholder's interests
2. Control and direct the organization
3. Create and deliver values
4. Be accountable for performance and compliance

Laws, regulations, and the organization's charters and bylaws determine the powers, duties, and responsibilities of the board of directors. **Charters** are written to initiate organizations, bodies, units, or initiatives, while **bylaws** define the internal organizational structure and governance rules. **Articles of incorporation** are a good example of a charter filed to create the organization as a legal entity.

Independent Director

When it comes to corporations, an independent director (also known as an outside director) is a director who does not have a material or pecuniary relationship with the company and must not be an officer or employee of the company or its subsidiaries.

For example, in 2002, the Sarbanes-Oxley Act (SOX) required that the **audit**, **compensation**, and **governance** committees be composed solely of **outside directors**.

Board-Level Committees

A committee is "a group of people appointed for a specific function, typically consisting of members of a larger group." (Google Dictionary)

The board of directors typically comprises a couple of committees. Some of them are mandatory because of legal or regulatory requirements. For example, the audit committee is the most common one required by the laws or regulations around the globe.

There are two types of board committees in terms of the life cycle: **standing** and **ad hoc** committees. Standing committees operate on a continual basis, while ad hoc committees are formed for a limited period of time to address a specific need.

Committees can be created at different levels of an organization and for various purposes. They can be organized at the project, management, or board level, or created for different purposes, such as steering, advisory, decision-making, operating, etc.

Steering Committees

A steering committee is "a committee that decides on the priorities or order of business of an organization and manages the general course of its operations." (Google Dictionary)

Board-level committees are typically composed of board members or directors. The purpose of steering committees (or task forces and advisory councils) is to involve **non-board members** in the board's work.

Common Board Committees

The following diagram represents the distribution of committees in the period 2001 to 2013. (Chen & Wu, 2016)

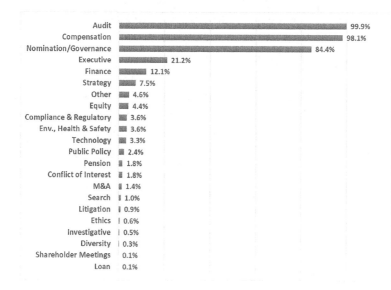

FIGURE 3-9 BOARD-LEVEL COMMITTEES

The following table is a summary of prevalent board-level committees:

Committee	Purpose
Audit Committee	The audit committee oversees the integrity and compliance of the firm's financial reporting.
Compensation Committee	The compensation committee focuses on human resource policies and procedures, most notably the compensation of top executives.
Governance Committee	The governance committee recommends new candidates for the board and other top executive positions and sets general governance procedures; directors are usually assigned to committees at the recommendation of the governance committee
Executive Committee	An executive committee is organized and delegated to represent the full board because it's not always practical for board members, especially large boards, to gather in-person to make decisions and take some necessary action. The executive committee is a standing committee, often functioning as a steering committee and composed of senior-level executives and board officers, such as the chair, the CEO, and a subset of officers and directors, to act on behalf of the board when the entire board cannot meet.

TABLE 3-1 COMMON BOARD-LEVEL COMMITTEES

C-Suite Executives

Officer	Description
CEO	• The Chief Executive Officer (CEO) is the highest-ranking officer. • The CEO makes high-level decisions about policy and strategy and reports to the board of directors.
COO	• The chief operating officer (COO) oversees the day-to-day administrative and operational functions. • The COO is the second-ranking officer who typically reports directly to the CEO.
CFO	• The Chief Financial Officer (CFO) oversees cash flow, financial planning, and taxation issues. • It is the third-highest position next to the CEO and COO.
CIO	• The Chief Information Officer (CIO) is the head of the IT department. The CIO may not report to the CEO directly, instead, CFO or COO. • Traditionally, it is common for the CIO to assume the CISO role.
CLO	• The Chief Legal Officer (CLO), general counsel, or chief counsel is the chief lawyer of a legal department. • The CLO or general counsel position is getting prominent in multinational companies, often directly advising the board of directors in place of outside lawyers.

TABLE 3-2 C-SUITE EXECUTIVES

Risk Function and CRO

In the government, "the risk executive is a functional role established within organizations to provide a more comprehensive, organization-wide approach to risk management. Heads of agencies or organizations may choose to retain the risk executive (function) or to delegate the function. The risk executive (function) can be filled by a single individual or office (supported by an expert staff) or by a designated group (e.g., a risk board, executive steering committee, executive leadership council)." (NIST SP 800-39)

The Chief Risk Officer (CRO) is an emerging role for big global companies since James Lam, the inventor of the ERM model became the first CRO at GE Capital in 1993. He managed credit risks, market risk, risk transfer, and hedge risk. The CRO is responsible for overseeing the organizational risk management and can advise the CEO and the board of directors.

Security Function and CISO

An organizational unit or department may perform one or more functions. For example, the HR function conducts staffing, development, compensation, safety and health, employee and labor relations, and so forth.

Security function ensures security by applying safeguards to protect assets from threats to achieve confidentiality, integrity, and availability. It can be a functional role filled by a non-security part (e.g., CIO); it also can be a formal organization unit lead by a Chief Information Security Officer (CISO), which is an emerging senior-level executive. As the head of information security, the CISO is responsible for overseeing and developing information security strategies, policies, and programs. The CISO may report to the CEO or other officers such as COO, CIO, CFO, etc.

3.3.5   ORGANIZATIONAL PROCESSES

Information security supports the mission and business of the organization. It is considered an embedded element in every organizational process and activity and requires a comprehensive and integrated approach.

A **process** is a "set of interrelated or interacting activities which transforms inputs into outputs." Porter's value chain divides value activities into two categories: primary and support activities. Every activity either creates values (directly or indirectly) or provides quality assurance.

This book treats high-level activities in the value chain as processes and introduces two of them mentioned in the CISSP CBK: **human resources** and **procurement (supply chain)**.

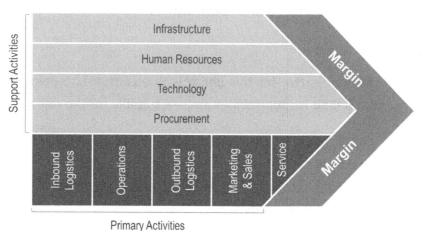

FIGURE 3-10 PORTER'S VALUE CHAIN

Human Resources

Human resources are the most critical assets of an organization. Organizations always do their best to build their employer brand and culture to attract the best candidates, recruit people through various channels, provide an engaging employee experience, foster ongoing professional development, retain top talents, and continue good morale when employees leave.

However, people are also the weakest link in the security chain. Security in human resources is also known as **personnel security**, which addresses security concerns by implementing security controls in each phase of the employee lifecycle.

For example, ISO 27001 deals with human resource security in three phases: prior to employment, during employment, and termination and change of employment.

Prior to employment

The control objective for this phase is to ensure that employees understand their responsibilities and are suitable for the roles.

- Background checks on all candidates shall be carried out and shall be proportional to the business requirements.
- The contractual agreements shall state responsibilities for information security.

During employment

The control objective for this phase is to ensure that employees are aware of and fulfill their information security responsibilities.

- Management shall require all employees to apply information security per the policies and procedures.

- All employees shall receive appropriate awareness training and education, and regular updates in policies and procedures.
- The disciplinary process shall be in place.

Termination and change of employment

The control objective for this phase is to protect the organization's interests.

- Information security responsibilities and duties that remain valid after termination or change of employment shall be defined, communicated to the employee, and enforced.

The following table summarizes HR-related security controls in terms of a 6-stage employee lifecycle:

Stage	Security Controls
Attraction	• Job design and job description
Recruitment	• Reference check • Interviewing • Background investigations
Onboarding	• Employment agreement • Non-disclosure agreement (NDA) • Non-competition agreement (NCA) • Acceptable use policy (AUP) • Privacy policy • Orientation
Development	• Job rotation • Cross-training
Retention	• Mandatory vacation • Periodic reinvestigation
Separation	• Exit interview • Escorted leave

TABLE 3-3 HR-RELATED SECURITY CONTROLS

Procurement and Supply Chain

An information system, its constituent components, and related Information and Communications Technology (ICT) products and services are either constructed in-house, acquired from external entities, or both.

Security engineering is the discipline that addresses security issues across the **system development life cycle** no matter the whole system or any of its components is **made** or **bought**. Building a system component involves a **development life cycle** (e.g., software development life cycle), as a portion of the system development life cycle, while acquiring one comprises a **procurement life cycle** as well. The following diagram is the system development life cycle (SDLC) introduced in NIST SP 800-64 R2.

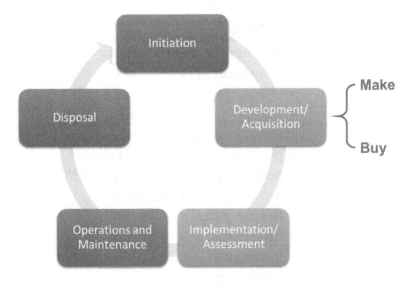

FIGURE 3-11 NIST SYSTEM DEVELOPMENT LIFE CYCLE

Procurement

Procurement is the process of obtaining a system, product, or service. It includes all stages of the process of acquiring product or services, beginning with the process for determining the need for the product or services and ending with contract completion and closeout.

The following is a general procurement life cycle:

1. Needs identification
2. Procurement planning
3. Requirement definition
4. Tendering or sourcing
5. Evaluation and selection
6. Contract award
7. Contract management

Supply Chain

Procurement relies on a complex, globally distributed, and interconnected supply chain and typically consists of multiple tiers of outsourcing, that is, an organization can subcontract activities to an external organization.

A supply chain is a linked set of resources and processes between multiple tiers of suppliers or vendors. The longer the supply chain is, the higher the risk. As a result, the supply chain risk must be considered and managed to enforce information security. Supply Chain Risk Management (SCRM) is the process of identifying, assessing, and mitigating the risks associated with the global and distributed nature of supply chains.

Service Level Agreement

A contract buying services from an external service provider typically outlines the services provided, duration, cost, resources, approach, assumptions, etc. The services provided by the service provider are defined in detail in a service level agreement (SLA). A service level agreement defines expectations of performance, describes measurable outcomes, and responds to identified instances of noncompliance. It focuses on the performance measurement and service quality agreed by both parties and can be used as a measurement tool as part of the contract.

A service level agreement can be part of a contract or a separate document. The rationale for having a separate SLA document is that the SLA can be revised without having to alter the contract. For example, the contract might last for one year, but the SLA may be reviewed and revised quarterly. The following are examples of service level requirements:

- The service availability shall be at least 99.999% (five nines) of any given month.
- A service report shall be provided monthly, or the requested information shall be provided within 3 hours after a request.

Foreign Ownership, Control, or Influence (FOCI)

Foreign ownership, control, or influence (FOCI) is a supply chain concern that the degree of ownership, control, or influence over a contractor by a foreign entity is as strong such that information security may be compromised. It is exceptionally substantial to national security, as defined in 32 CFR § 117.56.

Trust Relationship with Partners

Organizations can use trust models to evaluate the levels of trust needed when considering forming partnerships, collaborating with other organizations, sharing information, or receiving services.

There are five trust models: validated trust model, direct historical trust model, mediated trust model, mandated trust model, and hybrid trust model.

The following table is an excerpt from NIST SP 800-39:

Model	Feature
Validated Trust Model	In the validated trust model, one organization obtains a body of evidence regarding the actions of another organization (e.g., the organization's information security policies, activities, and risk-related decisions) and uses that evidence to establish a level of trust with the other organization.
Direct Historical Trust Model	In the direct historical trust model, the track record exhibited by an organization in the past, particularly in its risk and information security-related activities and decisions, can contribute to and help establish a level of trust with other organizations.
Mediated Trust Model	In the mediated trust model, an organization establishes a level of trust with another organization based on assurances provided by some mutually trusted third party.
Mandated Trust Model	In the mandated trust model, an organization establishes a level of trust with another organization based on a specific mandate issued by a third party in a position of authority.
Hybrid Trust Model	In general, the trust models described above are not mutually exclusive. Each of the trust models may be used independently as a stand-alone model or in conjunction with another model.

TABLE 3-4 TRUST MODELS

3.4   RISK MANAGEMENT

3.4.1   WHAT IS RISK MANAGEMENT?

Definition

> *Risk management is a systematic approach to frame, assess, respond, monitor, and communicate risk to control risk to a level **acceptable** to the management, contribute to the achievement of objectives, and create and protect value.*

Objectives and Risks

Risk is the "effect of uncertainty on **objectives**." In other words, a risk is any event, condition, or anything that affects the achievement of objectives, so it is in vain to talk about risk without any objectives in mind.

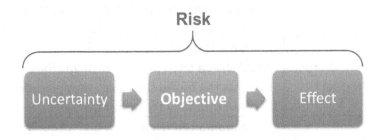

FIGURE 2-6 RISK FACTORS

There's an objective; there's a risk. Every organization exists to create and deliver values to its stakeholders as a goal or ultimate objective. However, the **objective** is subject to **risks** affecting its achievement. Organizational objectives are represented in different ways and granularity, such as mission, vision, goals, or intended outcomes, needs, or requirements, to name a few. Whenever we are talking about objectives, there comes risks and vice versa.

Controlling Risk to an Acceptable Level

- **Risk Exposure** is the potential loss presented to an individual, project, or organization by a risk. (ISO 16085:2006)
- **Risk Tolerance** is the acceptable level of **variation** that management is willing to allow for any particular risk as the enterprise pursues its objectives. (ISACA, 2019)
- **Risk Threshold** is the level of risk exposure **above** which risks are addressed and **below** which risks may be accepted. (PMBOK Guide — Sixth Edition)
- **Risk Treatment** is the process to eliminate risk or reduce it to a tolerable level. (ISO 15026-3:2015)
- **Risk Appetite** is the amount and type of risk that an organization is **willing** to pursue or retain. (ISO, 2009)
- **Risk Capacity** refers to the maximum amount of risk that an organization is **able** to endure.

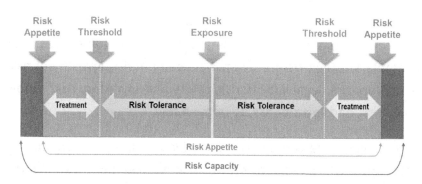

FIGURE 3-12 RISK CAPACITY AND RISK APPETITE

Enterprise Risk Management

Integrated, enterprise-wide risk management typically includes consideration of:

- The strategic goals/objectives of organizations (Tier 1)
- Organizational missions/business functions (Tier 1)

- Mission/business processes (Tier 2)
- Enterprise and information security architectures (Tier 2)
- System development life cycle processes (Tier 3)

FIGURE 3-13 RISKS AT DIFFERENT TIERS

3.4.2 Risk Category

Sources and Types of Risk

Organizations manage various **types** of risks emerging from different **tiers** in the organization to achieve **objectives**. For example, strategic risk, program management risk, investment risk, budgetary risk, legal liability risk, safety risk, inventory risk, supply chain risk, and security risk, to name a few.

To manage these various risks effectively, it is a good practice to **categorize** risks and adopt proven **risk management frameworks** to manage them.

Risk Taxonomy

As a risk may come from different **tiers** (information systems, mission/business processes, or organization) or originate from different **functions/departments** (e.g., human resources, finance, manufacturing, supply chains, etc.), to group or aggregate related risks or risk types into a broad category helps to manage risk and provide an integrated, organization-wide view for managing risk view.

A risk taxonomy is the (typically hierarchical) categorization of risk types. There is no over-arching risk taxonomy that applies consistently in a single industry or across industries. (Open Risk Manual contributors, 2019)

The following diagram from ISACA demonstrates common enterprise risk types and the dependency upon information technologies (IT):

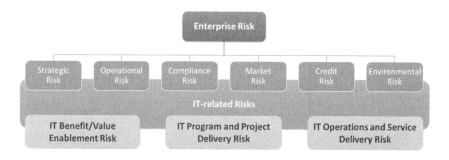

FIGURE 3-14 ENTERPRISE RISK TYPES

Strategic Risk

Strategic risk is related to the decisions about an organization's business strategy and strategic objectives, such as business model, competition, economic trends, reputation, consumer demand, M&A, and so on.

Operational Risk

Operational risk affects an organization's ability to execute its strategic plan because of the deficiency or issues of **people**, **systems**, and **processes**, such as fraud, security, privacy, human resources, supply chain, or physical risks.

Compliance Risk

Compliance risk relates to forced adherence to a law, regulation, standard, contract, rule, process, or practice. SOX, GLBA, GDPR, PCI-DSS, and ISO 27001 are regular compliance requirements.

Market Risk

Market risk, also called systematic risk, refers to the risk that is inherent from the entire market and affects everyone. For instance, interest rate risk, equity risk, currency risk, or exchange-rate risk are typical risks in the finance sector.

Credit Risks

Credit risk is the possibility of a loss resulting from a borrower's failure to repay a loan or meet contractual obligations. (Labarre, 2019)

Environmental Risks

Environmental Risks are related to the contribution an entity makes to climate change through greenhouse gas emissions, along with waste management and energy efficiency. Given renewed efforts to combat global warming, cutting emissions and decarbonizing have become more important. (Robeco, 2020)

IT-related risk

IT-related risks arise from legal liability or business loss due to, but not limited to, unauthorized (malicious, non-malicious, or accidental) disclosure, modification, or destruction of information, non-malicious errors and omissions, IT disruptions due to natural or human-made disasters, or failure to exercise due care and diligence in the implementation and operation of the IT.

3.4.3   RISK MANAGEMENT FRAMEWORKS

Definition

> *A risk management framework is a structured approach used to oversee and manage risk for an enterprise. (CNSSI 4009-2015)*

The following diagram shows the risk management frameworks introduced in this book. ISO 27005 and NIST FARM are introduced in Chapter 5 Information Security Risk management.

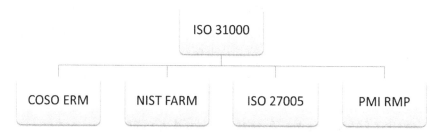

FIGURE 3-15 COMMON RISK MANAGEMENT FRAMEWORKS

ISO 31000

ISO 31000 is a generic risk management framework that provides definitions and terms, principles, and reference frameworks and processes. It treats risk as **neutral** - a risk is either a **threat** or **opportunity**.

This book adopts ISO 31000 as the ultimate foundation of risk management that applies to all types of risks at every tier and function.

COSO ERM

The Committee of Sponsoring Organizations of the Treadway Commission (COSO) Enterprise Risk Management - Integrated Framework, or COSO ERM for short, deals with **strategic**,

operational, reporting, compliance, environmental, social, governance risk, and so forth.

PMI RMP

The Project Management Institute (PMI) Risk Management Professional (RMP) certification introduces a risk management approach at the **project** level.

ISO 27005

ISO 27005 is the standard of information security risk management that complements ISO 27001 (information security management systems). ISO 27005 is a framework for **information risk**.

NIST FARM

The NIST FARM (**Frame, Assess, Respond**, and **Monitor**) provides a 3-tier approach that primarily addresses risk from the perspective of **information systems, business**, and **organization**.

3.4.4 ISO 31000

The international standard, **ISO 31000:2018 Risk management —
Guidelines**, provides guidelines on managing risk faced by
organizations but does not define certification requirements for
risk management. It includes **definitions and terms**, **principles**, and
recommendations for establishing a risk management **framework**
and **process** but does not include detailed instructions on risk
management or advice relevant to any specific domain.

The following are related standards:

- ISO Guide 73:2009 on Risk management – Vocabulary
- ISO 31004:2013 on Risk management – Guidance for the
  implementation of ISO 31000
- ISO 31010:2009 on Risk management – Risk assessment
  techniques

Risk management of ISO 31000 is driven by **values** that are realized
by the achievement of **objectives**. In other words, managing risk is
managing the effect of uncertainty on objectives to create and
protect values, that is directed by a set of **principles**, based on a
robust management **framework**, and following a defined **process**.

FIGURE 3-16 ISO 31000 CORE CONCEPTS

Definitions and Terms

There have been different perspectives and definitions of risk. It is common for people to think about risk as a danger, threat, or anything with negative consequences.

However, ISO 31000 defines risk as the **"effect of uncertainty on objectives."** An effect is a deviation from the expected. It can be positive, negative, or both, and can address, create, or result in opportunities and threats.

It is the **concept of neutral risk** introduced in this book that risk may lead to opportunities and threats, depending on its effect.

Risk Management Principles

The purpose of risk management is the creation and protection of value. Effective risk management requires risk management principles, as the following diagram shows.

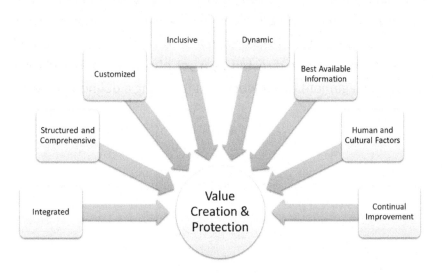

FIGURE 3-17 ISO 31000 RISK MANAGEMENT PRINCIPLES

Risk management should be **inclusive** to engage as broad stakeholders as possible. It should be **integrated** into all organization functions and activities and implemented based on a **structured and comprehensive** approach. Risk management framework and process are established and **customized** to meet the organization's and stakeholder's needs. **Best available information** informs decisions so that organizations can respond to risk timely and effectively in **dynamic** environments. **Human and cultural factors** influence all aspects of risk management across the organization and management cycles. **Continual improvement** through learning and experience is a crucial part of risk management.

Risk Management Framework

The purpose of the risk management framework is to assist the organization in integrating risk management into significant activities and functions.

FIGURE 3-18 ISO 31000 RISK MANAGEMENT FRAMEWORK

Risk Management Process

ISO 31000 introduces a generic risk management process as follows:

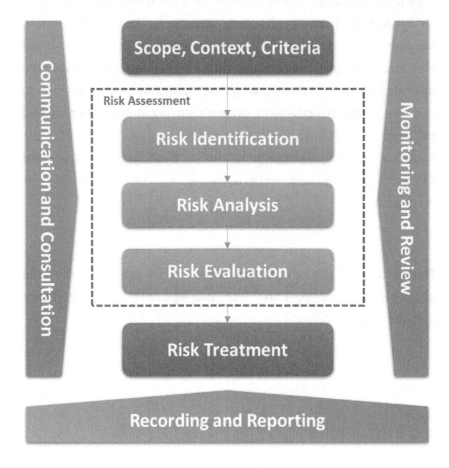

FIGURE 3-19 ISO 31000 RISK MANAGEMENT PROCESS

Scope, context, and criteria

As risk arises from different organizational functions or levels (e.g., strategic, operational, program, project, or other activities), it is important to be clear about the scope of risk management.

The external and internal context is the environment in which the organization seeks to define and achieve its objectives.

The organization should specify the amount and type of risk that it may or may not take, relative to objectives.

It should also define criteria to evaluate the significance of risk and to support decision-making processes. risk criteria should be established at the beginning of the risk assessment process.

A risk might happen or materialize and cause loss. The expected value of the loss is called **risk exposure**. It may incur as one of the costs of the pursuit of objectives for values; that is, managing risks has a price, so risk management should be **cost-effective**.

Risk Identification

Risk has to be identified to be managed. Risk identification is the process of finding and recognizing uncertainties that may affect the **objectives** and describing them structurally.

Relevant, appropriate, and up-to-date information is important in identifying risks. Any risk found must be relevant to objectives; otherwise, it is not a risk.

The following practices complement ISO 31000:

- Identified Risks are recorded in the **risk register**.
- The **risk owner** accountable for each risk is assigned at the stage of risk identification.
- An identified risk without any treatment or handling is called **inherent risk**, raw risk, or native risk.

Risk Analysis

Risk analysis decomposes risk into discrete risk factors and determines the risk exposure. Risk can be described and comprehended by a risk model that comprises a variety of risk factors such as uncertainty (e.g., risk source, event, vulnerability, likelihood, possibility, or cause) and effect (e.g., impact, consequence, or ramification).

Risk exposure is typically determined by **uncertainty** and **effect**. It can be presented with **monetary value**, **score**, or **level** (e.g., high, moderate, or low), depending on the analysis approach – **qualitative** or **quantitative**.

The qualitative analysis relies on **subjective** intuition, experience, and judgment. Interview, Delphi method, and scenario analysis are common qualitative analysis techniques.

The quantitative analysis emphasizes **objective** data, facts, or evidence. Time series analysis, regression analysis, and Monte Carlo simulation are conventional quantitative analysis techniques.

ISO 31000 distinguishes risk analysis from **risk assessment**, which stands for risk identification, risk analysis, and risk evaluation collectively. Risk analysis is part of risk assessment. However, they are commonly used interchangeably in other frameworks.

Risk Evaluation

The purpose of risk evaluation is to support decisions. Risk evaluation determines which risks require further actions or treatment by comparing the results of the risk analysis with the established risk criteria.

Risk exposure determined in risk analysis is the basis of **risk prioritization** so that organizations can decide which risks should be handled and which are retained or left intact. If the risk exposure exceeds the **risk tolerance**, risk should be handled.

Risk evaluation is a standalone activity in ISO 31000. However, it may be integrated into risk analysis in other frameworks.

Risk Treatment

The purpose of risk treatment is to select and implement options for addressing risk. Risk treatment may involve one or more options as they are not necessarily mutually exclusive or appropriate in all circumstances. The term risk treatment is commonly used interchangeably with risk response (project risk) or risk handling (general usage).

Options for treating risk may involve one or more of the following:

1. **Avoiding** the risk of removing the **risk source**
2. Taking or increasing the risk to pursue an **opportunity**;
3. **Modifying** risk by changing the **likelihood** or **consequences**
4. **Sharing** the risk (e.g., through contracts, buying insurance)
5. **Retaining** the risk by informed decision

Risk treatment is an iterative process as follows:

1. Formulate and select risk treatment options
2. Plan and implement risk treatment
3. Assess the effectiveness of the treatment implemented
4. Decide whether the remaining or residual risk is acceptable
5. If not acceptable, take further treatment

Risk treatment should be justified by considering cost/benefit, the organization's objectives, obligations, risk criteria, available resources, stakeholders, and so forth.

Risk treatment can also introduce new risks, also known as secondary risks, that need to be managed.

The risk exposure after risk treatment is called **residual risk**. The management decides if the residual risk is accepted based on their **risk appetite**. Risk exposure exceeds the **risk threshold** will not be accepted.

Communication and consultation

The purpose of communication and consultation is to assist relevant stakeholders in understanding risk, the basis on which decisions are made, and the reasons why particular actions are required.

Monitoring and Review

Risk should be monitored and reviewed continuously. If the risk exposure exceeds the **risk tolerance**, risk treatment should be implemented.

Monitoring and review should take place in all stages of the process. Monitoring and review include planning, gathering and analyzing information, recording results, and providing feedback.

The results of monitoring and review should be incorporated throughout the organization's performance management, measurement, and reporting activities.

Recording and reporting

The risk management process and its outcomes should be documented and reported through appropriate mechanisms.

3.4.5   COSO ERM

The Committee of Sponsoring Organizations of the Treadway Commission (COSO), initially formed in 1985, is a joint initiative of five private sector organizations and is dedicated to providing thought leadership through the development of comprehensive frameworks and guidance on **enterprise risk management (ERM)**, **internal control**, and **fraud deterrence**. COSO's supporting organizations are the Institute of Internal Auditors (IIA), the American Accounting Association (AAA), the American Institute of Certified Public Accountants (AICPA), Financial Executives International (FEI), and the Institute of Management Accountants (IMA).

COSO Publications

Sound risk management and internal control are necessary for the long-term success of all organizations. COSO published two primary frameworks and guidance and papers as supplements.

- Enterprise Risk Management – Integrating with Strategy and Performance in 2017, and
- Internal Control – Integrated Framework in 2013.

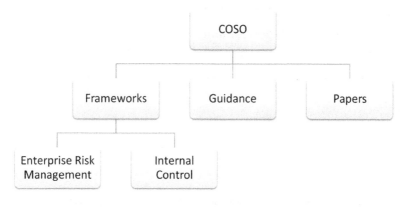

FIGURE 3-20 COSO PUBLICATIONS

COSO ERM

Enterprise risk management is a process, to provide reasonable assurance regarding the achievement of entity **objectives**, which is:

- effected by an entity's board of directors, management and other personnel
- applied in strategy setting and across the enterprise, and
- designed to identify potential events that may affect the entity, and manage risk to be within its **risk appetite**.

This enterprise risk management framework is geared to achieving an entity's objectives, set forth in four categories:

- Strategic: high-level goals, aligned with and supporting its mission
- Operations: effective and efficient use of its resources
- Reporting: reliability of reporting
- Compliance: compliance with applicable laws and regulations.

COSO ERM Features

The COSO ERM focuses on integration with the **business model** to result in better information, support improved decision-making, and lead to enhanced performance.

FIGURE 3-21 ENTERPRISE RISK MANAGEMENT TIED TO THE BUSINESS MODEL

The COSO ERM provides 20 principles that closely tie to the business model. It emphasizes value, recognizes the importance of culture, and builds links to strategy, performance, and internal control.

Business Model Steps	Principles
Mission, Vision & Core Values	1. Exercises Board Risk Oversight 2. Establishes Operating Structures 3. Defines Desired Culture 4. Demonstrates Commitment to Core Values 5. Attracts, Develops and Retains Capable Individuals
Strategy Development	6. Analyzes Business Context 7. Defines Risk Appetite 8. Evaluates Alternative Strategies 9. Formulates Business Objectives
Business Objectives Formulation	10. Identifies Risk 11. Assesses Severity of Risk 12. Prioritizes Risk 13. Implements Risk Responses 14. Develops Portfolio View
Implementation & Performance	15. Assesses Substantial Change 16. Reviews Risk and Performance 17. Pursues Improvement in Enterprise Risk Management
Enhanced Value	18. Leverages Information and Technology 19. Communicates Risk Information 20. Reports on Risk, Culture, and Performance

TABLE 3-5 COSO ERM PRINCIPLES

COSO ERM - Internal control

The COSO ERM consists of eight interrelated components. Internal control is an integral part of enterprise risk management.

Internal control is a process incorporated in enterprise risk management, effected by an entity's board of directors, management, and other personnel and designed to provide reasonable assurance of the achievement of **objectives** in the following categories: 1) effectiveness and efficiency of operations and 2) reliability of financial reporting.

ERM Components	Internal Control Principles
Control Environment	1. Demonstrates commitment to integrity and ethical values 2. Exercises oversight responsibility 3. Establishes structure, authority, and responsibility 4. Demonstrates commitment to competence 5. Enforces accountability
Risk Assessment	6. Specifies suitable objectives 7. Identifies and analyzes risk 8. Assesses fraud risk 9. Identifies and analyzes the significant change
Control Activities	10. Selects and develops control activities 11. Selects and develops general controls over technology 12. Deploys through policies and procedures
Information & Communication	13. Uses relevant information 14. Communicates internally 15. Communicates externally
Monitoring	16. Conducts ongoing and/or separate evaluations 17. Evaluates and communicates deficiencies

TABLE 3-6 COSO INTERNAL CONTROL PRINCIPLES

COSO ERM - Risk Assessment

Risk assessment of COSO ERM lies between risk identification and risk response, just as the ISO 31000 does. Its purpose is to determine the risk exposure to measure how significant the risks are and prioritize them so that the management can focus on the most critical threats and opportunities and respond to risks effectively.

The COSO ERM Paper, <u>Risk Assessment in Practice</u>, has details. It can be downloaded from the COSO web site (https://coso.org).

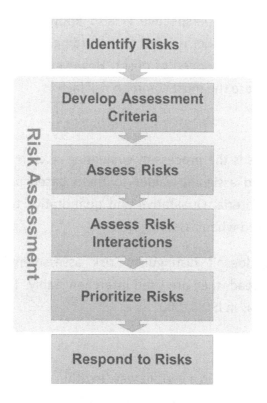

FIGURE 3-22 COSO ERM RISK ASSESSMENT

Identify Risks

The risk identification process produces a comprehensive list of risks from different sources of business units, corporate functions, and projects, making up the enterprise's risk profile.

Develop Assessment Criteria

Defining risk-related criteria are defined at the context establishment stage in ISO 31000, while it is part of risk assessment in COSO ERM.

Assessment criteria are used to evaluate risk from various perspectives. Each perspective is also known as a risk factor. Organizations can tailor risk factors according to their needs, such as vulnerability and speed of onset. However, the likelihood and impact of risk are the most common risk factors.

Assess Risks

Assessing risks is the process of evaluating risks in terms of each risk factor and assigning values to them based on the defined assessment criteria. Qualitative and quantitative techniques are commonly used when assessing risks.

COSO ERM doesn't distinguish "risk assessment" from "risk analysis." Instead, they are used interchangeably. This step maps the risk analysis in ISO 31000.

Assess Risk Interactions

Risks are correlated in a certain way. In other words, they interact with one another. They can be grouped and then assigned a risk owner to break down silos and manage them with a holistic view. Risk interaction maps, correlation matrices, aggregated probability distributions, and bow-tie diagrams are tools for capturing risk relationships.

Prioritize risks

Risk prioritization is the process of determining risk management priorities by comparing the risk exposure against predetermined criteria and subjective judgment. This is the last step of risk assessment. Its results then serve as the input to risk responses.

This step maps the risk evaluation in ISO 31000.

Respond to Risks

Risk response options, such as accept, reduce, share, or avoid, are examined with the consideration of cost-benefit. Once response options are selected, a response strategy is formulated, and risk response plans are developed.

3.4.6   PMI RMP

Information risk should be considered at the project level as well. When implementing Information Security Management System (ISMS), information security at the project level is also a requirement of ISO 27001 Annex A, which states, "Information security shall be addressed in project management, regardless of the type of the project."

The PMBOK Guide defines project risk as "an **uncertain** event or condition that, if it occurs, has a positive or negative **effect** on a project's **objectives**." Project objectives include scope, schedule, cost, and quality. The following diagram depicts the project risk management process introduced in the book, "Practice Standard for Project Risk Management," and adopted by the PMI Risk Management Professional (RMP) certification. The defined steps of the project risk management process describe a structured approach for understanding and managing risk on a project.

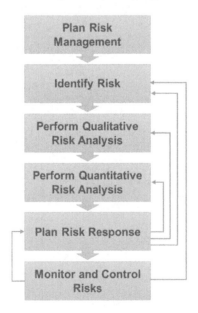

FIGURE 3-23 PROJECT RISK MANAGEMENT PROCESS

Project Risk Management Process

Key points in each step are summarized in the following table. Please refer to PMI's publication <u>Practice Standard for Project Risk Management</u> for details.

Step	Key Points
Plan Risk Management	<ul><li>Tailored risk management processes</li><li>Risk thresholds</li><li>Process rules</li><li>Risk management plan</li></ul>
Identify Risks	<ul><li>List of risks</li><li>Risk owners</li></ul>
Perform Qualitative Risk Analysis	<ul><li>Probability</li><li>Impact</li><li>Root causes</li><li>Importance</li><li>Prioritized list</li></ul>
Perform Quantitative Risk Analysis	<ul><li>Numerical models</li><li>Combined outcomes</li><li>Confidence limits</li><li>Sensitivity analysis</li><li>Prioritized list updates</li></ul>
Plan Risk Responses	<ul><li>Strategies</li><li>Actions</li><li>Action owners</li><li>Timing</li><li>Analysis</li><li>Project plan updates</li></ul>
Monitor and Control Risks	<ul><li>Status and trends</li><li>Reporting</li><li>Trends in risk exposure</li></ul>

TABLE 3-7 PROJECT RISK MANAGEMENT PROCESS

3.5 COMPLIANCE

Definitions

> **Compliance** *is the fulfillment of specified requirements. (ISO 2394)*
>
> **Conformance** *is the fulfillment of specified requirements. (ISO 19105)*
>
> **Conformity** *is the fulfillment of a requirement. (ISO 22301)*

The definitions of compliance and conformance are literally identical, but some consider compliance as **forced adherence** but conformance as **voluntary adherence**. However, this book does not rigorously distinguish the two. **Conformity** is a related concept that emphasizes the fulfillment of a **"single"** requirement.

Compliance is one of the most significant risk sources. This book broadly divides compliance requirements into two levels: organization and individual.

- **Organization-level** compliance requirements apply to the organization, such as laws and regulations, industry standards, contracts. Most of them are specific and explicit.
- **Individual-level** compliance requirements primarily apply to employees or individuals, such as organizational policies, due care/due diligence, and ethics. Some of them are generic and implicit.

Organization Level

Laws & Regulations

Industry Standards

Contracts

Individual Level

Organizational Policies

Due Care/Due Diligence

Ethics

FIGURE 3-24 COMPLIANCE CONCERNS

3.5.1   Organizational Level

Laws and Regulations

Laws and regulations are similar in that both are mandatory requirements. However, there are some minute differences between them in terms of separation of powers or government structure. Generally speaking, laws refer to the rules written and passed by the legislative branch, while regulations are the rules formulated by the executive branch.

For example, US Federal laws are bills that have passed both houses of Congress and been signed by the president. Individual laws, also called acts, are arranged by subject in the United States Code (USC), e.g., Federal Information Security Management Act of 2002 (FISMA, 44 USC § 3541, et seq.).

Regulations are rules made by executive departments and agencies and arranged by subject in the Code of Federal Regulations (CFR), e.g., The HIPAA Security Rule is located at 45 CFR Part 160 and Subparts A and C of Part 164.

The following are some well-known laws and regulations:

- HIPAA defines security and privacy rules for the healthcare and healthcare insurance industries.
- HITECH updates many of HIPAA's privacy and security requirements and introduces new data breach notification requirements.
- GLBA removes market barriers among banking, securities, and insurance companies and allows them to consolidate. However, it defines financial privacy rules, safeguards rules, and requires pretexting protection to enforce information security.

- SOX has a profound effect on corporate governance because it requires public companies to enhance disclosure, strengthen audit committees and internal controls, and hold directors and officers personally liable for the accuracy of financial statements and establish stricter criminal penalties for fraud.
- GDPR addresses the transfer of personal data outside the European Union (EU). Controllers and processors of personal data are roles responsible for ensuring and implementing the data protection principles and measures. A mandatory role, data protection officer (DPO), is responsible for managing compliance with the GDPR.

Industry Standards

Organizations pursue compliance with industry standards because of management mandates, customer demands, market competition, or even the laws and regulations.

The following are some of the well-known standards:

- **ISO 27001 – Information Security Management System**. It is a universal international standard and applies to all organizations, regardless of type, size, or nature.
- **ISO 22301 – Business Continuity Management System**. It also applies to all types, sizes, and nature of organizations.
- **PCI DSS – Payment Card Industry Data Security Standard**. It is an information security standard for organizations that handle payment cards, such as Visa, MasterCard, American Express, etc. In other words, it applies to all entities that store, process, or transmit cardholder data.

Contracts

A contract is "a mutually binding legal relationship obligating the seller to furnish the supplies or services (including construction) and the buyer to pay for them." (48 CFR) In other words, a contract is an agreement between two or more parties intended to be enforceable by law.

Security-related contractual requirements by the seller may include but not limited to:

- Service level requirements
- Performance measurement requirements
- Minimum security requirements
- Contingency planning requirements
- Compliance with laws
- The right to audit
- Restrictions on disclosure to third parties
- Security breach procedures
- Return or destruction of personal information
- Indemnification

Even though PCI DSS is a standard for the payment card industry, it is the contract that enforces PCI DSS requirements applicable to the company accepting payment card transactions.

3.5.2   INDIVIDUAL LEVEL

Organizational Policies

According to ISO 22301, a policy stands for the "intentions and direction of an organization, as formally expressed by its top management." In other words, a policy is the **management intent** that directs organizational operations and affects people's behavior. A **policy framework** refers to the policy and its supporting standards, procedures, and guidelines.

Regulatory policies are typically set out to reflect newly effected laws or regulations. Developing and implementing policies is evidence of due care and due diligence on the part of senior management.

Due Diligence and Due Care

Due diligence is a **reasonable** amount of **careful** and **persistent** work or effort, and due care lies at the core of due diligence. Individuals, organizations, or even nations exercise **due diligence** to inform risk-based decision making to avoid loss and liability. Meanwhile, they also use **due care** to ensure the decision is made and implemented without negligence. **Negligence** is a failure to exercise the care that a reasonably prudent person would exercise under similar circumstances; that is, lack of due care.

Due care means "the degree of care that a prudent and competent person engaged in the same line of business or endeavor would exercise under similar circumstances. Due care does not permit willful ignorance." (16 CFR § 1107.2)

Due diligence can be part of the risk assessment process. People typically exercise due diligence, as a preemptive or proactive measure, by **checking things out** or **conducting investigations** to inform **risk-based decision making**.

As due diligence focuses on risk-based decision making, it is more often, but not limited to, for the **management** to exercise due diligence than others. In contrast, **everybody** has to use due care to get things done without negligence.

Standard of Due Diligence

However, how much diligence or how diligent is enough to meet the standard of due diligence? There is no uniform or widely agreed standard, and it varies across professions or contexts. For example, in the context of a merger & acquisition case, the following professional due diligence may be performed:

- **Financial due diligence** may focus on uncovering any financial abnormalities.
- **Legal due diligence** may involve analyzing the company's agreements, licenses, ownership, and legal standing to operate.
- **Information security due diligence** may contain activities such as data leakage review, cyber health check, supply chain risk assessment, SDLC and DevOps evaluation, and so forth.

Security Operations Due Diligence

When it comes to security operations, according to the Official (ISC)² Guide to the CISSP CBK 4th edition, examples of due diligence for security professionals in an organization include but are not limited to:

- Background checks of employees

- Credit checks of business partners
- Information system security assessments
- Risk assessments of physical security systems
- Penetration tests of firewalls
- Contingency testing of backup systems
- Threat intelligence services being used to check on the availability of company Intellectual Property (IP)

The Official (ISC)² CISSP Study Guide states:

- **Due care** is using reasonable care to **protect** the interests of an organization.
- **Due diligence** is practicing the activities that **maintain** the due care effort.

If an organization does not practice due care and due diligence, the management can be held liable for negligence and held accountable for losses. Exercising careful and persistent endeavor to inform risk-based decision making and implementation demonstrates adequate due care and due diligence. It reduces the liability of the management when a loss occurs.

Ethics

Compliance and ethics go hand in hand. The organizational ethics program usually serves as part of internal controls and risk management. It identifies the boundary of laws and ethics and establishes a system to alert management when the organization is approaching or crossing the border.

Code of ethics, code of conduct, conflicts of interest, ethical culture, diversity of the workforce, blog and social networking, incentives, and whistleblower protections are common issues addressed in the ethics program.

3.5.3   SECURITY ASSESSMENT AND AUDIT

Laws and regulations, industry standards, contracts, organizational policies, due care/due diligence, and ethics are familiar sources of compliance requirements, but how do we know individuals and organizations are compliant with them? The answer is assessment and audit.

Assessment

An **assessment** is performed to evaluate the **fulfillment of specified requirements**; an **audit** is a formal assessment conducted by independent parties or auditors. In the context of information security, security assessments and audits are common practices.

SCA and ISA

Security assessment may refer to **security control assessment (SCA)** or **information security assessment (ISA)**. Security control assessment (SCA) is part of the information security assessment (ISA); they are similar but have different scope.

- A **security control assessment (SCA)** means "the testing or evaluation of **security controls** to determine the extent to which the controls are implemented correctly, operating as intended, and producing the desired outcome with respect to meeting the security requirements for an information system or organization." (NIST SP 800-53 R4)
- An **information security assessment (ISA)** is "the process of determining how effectively an **entity** being assessed (e.g., host, system, network, procedure, person—known as the assessment object) meets specific security objectives." (NIST SP 800-115)

Security Assessment

Security assessment generally refers to the evaluation applied to the information system, its components and environment, and the security controls that enforce security, through testing, examination, and interviewing.

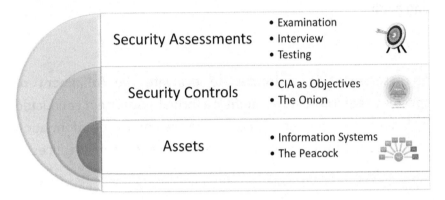

FIGURE 3-25 SECURITY ASSESSMENT

Assessment Methods

According to NIST SP 800-115, there are three typical types of assessment methods: testing, examination, and interviewing.

- **Testing** is the process of exercising one or more assessment objects under specified conditions to **compare actual and expected behaviors**.
- **Examination** is the process of checking, inspecting, reviewing, observing, studying, or analyzing one or more assessment objects to facilitate understanding, achieve clarification, or **obtain evidence**.
- **Interviewing** is the process of conducting discussions with individuals or groups within an organization to facilitate understanding, achieve clarification, or **identify the location of evidence**.

Audit

An audit is one type of independent assessment. ISO 19011 defines an audit as a "**systematic, independent** and **documented** process for obtaining audit **evidence** [records, statements of fact or other information which are relevant and verifiable] and evaluating it objectively to determine the extent to which the audit **criteria** [a set of policies, procedures or requirements] are fulfilled."

Audit Types

- **First-party audits**, also known as internal audits, are conducted by the internal audit function, e.g., the audit committee under the board of directors.
- **Second-party audits** are held against their proprietary requirements by external interested parties, e.g., first-tier customers.
- **Third-party audits** are performed against a recognized standard by independent external bodies, such as the big four (Deloitte, EY, KPMG, and PwC) or ISO certification bodies (BSI, SGS, TUV, etc.), generally accepted as the most robust type of assurance system.

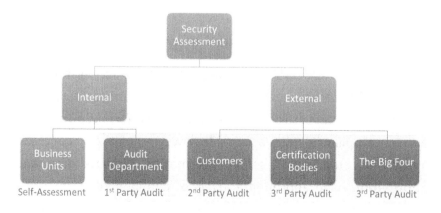

FIGURE 3-26 AUDIT PARTIES

Integrated Audit

An **integrated audit** considers the relationship between information technology, financial and operational controls in establishing an effective and efficient internal control environment. **Compliance audits** demonstrate adherence to specific regulatory or industry standards. The purpose of a **financial audit** is to assess the accuracy of financial reporting. An **operational audit** is designed to evaluate the internal control structure in a given process or area.

FIGURE 3-27 INTEGRATED AUDITS

According to ISACA CISA review manual, **Information Systems (IS) audit** is the formal examination, interview and/or testing of information systems to determine whether 1) **information systems** are in compliance with applicable laws, regulations, contracts and/or industry guidelines, 2) **information systems data and information** have appropriate levels of confidentiality, integrity, and availability, and 3) **information systems operations** are being accomplished efficiently, and effectiveness targets are being met.

Internal Security Assessment

An internal security assessment or self-assessment is not an audit because it is conducted by the staff and management of the organization or business units.

It is a management technique that assures stakeholders that the internal control system of the organization is reliable and ensures that employees are aware of the risk to the business, and they conduct periodic, proactive reviews of controls.

Service Organization Control (SOC) Reports

ISAE 3402, published by the IFAC, is an international assurance standard that prescribes Service Organization Control (SOC) report. SSAE 16, produced by the AICPA, mirrors the ISAE 3402.

- ISAE: International Standard on Assurance Engagements
- IFAC: International Federation of Accountants
- SSAE: Statement on Standards for Attestation Engagements
- AICPA: American Institute of Certified Public Accountants

Service Organization Control (SOC) reports, issued by independent third-party auditors, give assurance to a user entity that the service organization has adequate internal controls.

FIGURE 3-28 SERVICE ORGANIZATION CONTROL (SOC)

SOC reports are beneficial for:

- Corporate governance
- Compliance management
- Cybersecurity risk management program
- Cybersecurity risks in supply chains

There are two types of SOC reports, Type I and Type II.

Applicable...	Type I	Type II
Time	One point in time (snapshot)	One period of time (six months minimum)
Controls	Performed at least once	Performed over a period of time
Assessment	Walkthrough and Observation	Walkthrough, Observation, Sampling, and Testing
Justification	Customer requirements New controls implemented Unconfident in passing Type II	Customer requirements

FIGURE 3-29 TYPES OF SOC REPORTS

SOC reports can also be categorized into SOC-1, SOC-2, and SOC-3 in terms of audit standards and report users.

Applicable...	SOC-1	SOC-2	SOC-3
Standard	SSAE 18 AICPI Guide	AT 101 AICPI Guide	AT 101 Technical Practice Aid
Controls	Internal Control over Financial Reporting (ICFR)	Security/Systems, Privacy	Security/Systems, Privacy
Controls reference	N/A	Trusted Services Principles/GAPP	Trusted Services Principles/GAPP
Usage of report	User Auditor Management of SO Management of User	Knowledgeable parties	Anyone

FIGURE 3-30 SOC-1, SOC-2, AND SOC-3

REVIEW QUESTIONS

1. **Which of the following is not a concern of security function?**
   A. The position in the organizational structure
   B. The roles and responsibilities
   C. The reporting line of CISO
   D. The nomination of board members

2. **Which of the following roles oversees the integrity and compliance of the firm's financial reporting?**
   A. CFO
   B. CEO
   C. Audit committee
   D. The chairperson of the board

3. **Which of the following should be conducted at the separation stage of the employee life cycle?**
   A. Orientation
   B. Reference check
   C. Exit interview
   D. Mandatory vacation

4. **Which of the following stages of the NIST SDLC is procurement conducted?**
   A. Initiation
   B. Development/Acquisition
   C. Implementation/Assessment
   D. Operations and Maintenance

5. **Which of the following statements is true?**
   A. Risk always brings negative effects.
   B. Risk can be eliminated completely.
   C. Risk is the effect of uncertainty on objectives
   D. Risk and threat are synonyms

6. **Which of the following refers to the potential loss presented to an individual, project, or organization by a risk?**

   A. Risk exposure

   B. Risk appetite

   C. Risk tolerance

   D. Risk capacity

7. **Which of the following is not a risk management framework?**

   A. ISO 31000

   B. COSO ERM

   C. NIST FARM

   D. CMMI

8. **Which of the following is not part of risk assessment?**

   A. Risk analysis

   B. Risk treatment

   C. Risk evaluation

   D. Risk identification

9. **Which of the following is a general risk response strategy?**

   A. Risk attitude

   B. Risk appetite

   C. Risk acceptance

   D. Risk aversion

10. **Which of the following is not an assessment method?**

    A. Examination

    B. Interviewing

    C. Testing

    D. Audit

4 STRATEGIC MANAGEMENT

"Would you tell me, please,
which way I ought to go from here?"

- Lewis Carroll, Alice in Wonderland

4.1 WHAT IS STRATEGY?

Definition

> *A strategy is an **approach** or **overall plan** that points out the **direction** and entails **initiatives** to achieve long-term **goals**.*

The definition of strategy above is developed based on the following sources:

- **Plan** to achieve a **long-term** or **overall objective**. (ISO 9000:2015)
- **Plan** to accomplish the organization's **mission** and achieve the organization's **vision**. (ISO 21001:2018)
- Organization's **overall plan** of development, describing the effective use of **resources** in support of the organization in its future activities. Note 1 to entry: involves setting **objectives** and proposing **initiatives** for action. (ISO 24765:2017)
- Organization's **approach** to achieving its **objectives**. (ISO 30400:2016)

A strategy fulfills the organization's mission and vision and achieves long-term goals. This topic is introduced in 4.2.1 Strategic Thinking.

A strategy, also called a strategic plan comprises initiatives materialized into action plans or tactic plans. 4.2 Strategy Formulation and 4.3 Strategy Execution have more details.

4.1.1   LEVELS OF STRATEGY

Strategies can be developed at three levels: **corporate**, **business**, and **functional** level. The level of a strategy determines its scope. Strategy development usually takes a top-down approach. A strategy at a lower level should align with the upstream strategy or the one at the upper level.

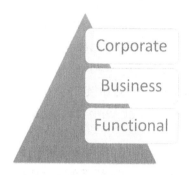

FIGURE 4-1 LEVELS OF STRATEGIES

Example Strategies

Strategy	Examples
Corporate Level	• Growth: acquisition, merger, and joint venture • Stability: pause/proceed with caution, no-change, and profit • Renewal: divestiture for survival, pivot to growth
Business Level	• Cost leadership • Differentiation • Market focus
Functional Level	• Pricing strategies: creaming or skimming, penetration pricing, price discrimination, and so forth • Branding strategies: product line extension, multi-brand, brand extension, new brand, and so on

TABLE 4-1 EXAMPLE STRATEGIES

4.1.2   STRATEGIC ALIGNMENT

Strategies at a lower level should be aligned with those at the upper level to create **strategic synergy**; that is, the integrated set of strategies as a whole produces more values than a bunch of discrete, unrelated, or even conflicting ones.

It is a typical scenario that the CEO or president plots a corporate-level strategy first. Subordinate chief officers or vice presidents then derive the business-level strategy, also known as competitive strategy, based on the upstream corporate strategy. Middle managers under each business unit then develop the function-level or functional strategy aligned with the business-level strategy.

For example, Microsoft's corporate strategy may denote an overall idea, e.g., growing through mergers and acquisitions (M&A). It may drive other chief officers and vice presidents to come up with business strategies such as Cloud-first/Mobile-first strategy, a strategy with a focus on augmented virtual reality (VR), Tech Intensity strategy, and so forth.

4.2   STRATEGY FORMULATION

Strategy formulation is the planning process of strategic thinking and strategic analysis to develop strategies that are composed of portfolios of projects.

Strategic thinking is envisioning for the future. The strategic analysis determines the current state and transforms the future state into strategic goals. Strategic planning develops a strategy or strategic plan to achieve the strategic goals and objectives and fulfill the vision and mission.

A strategic plan comprises a collection of initiatives. Each initiative has to be evaluated and justified by a business case to turn into a project. Projects are sponsored by the management and grouped into programs and portfolios to create strategic synergy.

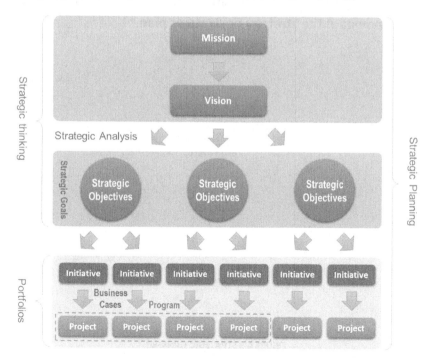

FIGURE 4-2 STRATEGY FORMULATION

4.2.1   STRATEGIC THINKING

Mission

Strategic thinking is the cognitive thinking process about the organization's existence, growth, and long-term development. The first step of strategic thinking starts from pondering the **purpose** and **values** of the organization and envisioning persistent success. Even though laws typically define the missions of government departments or agencies, it is common for organizations to state the purpose and values in the **mission statement**.

Vision

A **vision** is the picture of success where the purpose and values are satisfied. It is the future state described by a set of **intended outcomes** refactored into **strategic goals** to direct the development of the **strategy** or **strategic plan**.

FIGURE 4-3 STRATEGIC THINKING

Some may argue that vision should be defined before the mission. However, the opinions are inconsistent. So, it is not uncommon for organizations to merge the mission and vision into one statement, the mission or vision statement. This book assumes the mission goes first.

The following are examples of mission statements.

Microsoft

EMPOWERING OTHERS

Our mission is to empower every person and organization on the planet to achieve more.

https://www.microsoft.com/en-us/about

Amicliens

INSPIRE PEOPLE

Our mission is to inspire people and become a share point of people and knowledge.

FIGURE 4-4 AMICLIENS MISSION STATEMENT

4.2.2   STRATEGIC ANALYSIS

Strategic analysis is the process of assessing the **status quo** and determines **strategic goals**, in contrast to the strategic thinking of envisioning the **future**. It is a vital part of strategy formulation and driven by analyzing the **context** of the **organization** and the **needs** of **stakeholders**.

SWOT analysis is one of the most common techniques organizations used to analyze the external and internal environment, assess risks, and formulate strategies to seize opportunities and handle threats. The **SWOT Matrix** is a useful tool to guide the analysis work and demonstrate the result. An **external analysis** explores opportunities and threats in the macro-environment or the industry, while an **internal analysis** identifies the strengths and weaknesses of the organization. **Strategies** are formulated from the analysis results in the four quadrants.

There are many tools available for external and internal analysis. For example, **Porter's 5 Forces** is a well-known model for external analysis, while the **Value Chain** is for internal analysis.

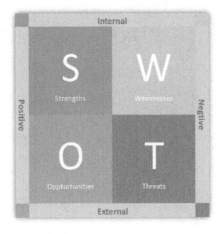

FIGURE 4-5 SWOT ANALYSIS

Strategic Goals and Objectives

Strategic goals can be derived from the vision and mission with the considerations of the result of SWOT analysis that entails organization's strengths and weaknesses, the external environment's opportunities and threats, stakeholder's expectations and needs, and other factors

Strategic goals are then refactored into strategic objectives. A **strategy map** introduced in the Balanced Scorecard (BSC) can be used to organize and visualize the strategic goals and objectives in a hierarchical manner and from different perspectives, such as financial, customer, internal business processes, and learning and growth. The following diagram depicts the Balanced Scorecard (BSC) presented in a strategy map, a hierarchy of perspectives composed of objectives (shown as ovals on the map) with a logical, cause-and-effect relationship.

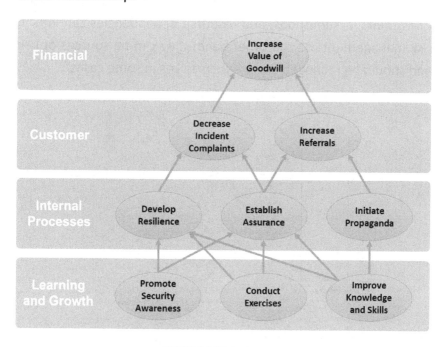

FIGURE 4-6 STRATEGY MAP

4.2.3 STRATEGIC PLANNING

Strategic planning is the process whereby a strategy is developed to achieve the strategic goals and fulfill the vision and mission. A **strategy** is an approach or high-level plan that points out the direction to achieve the strategic goals derived from the vision and mission and can be formulated with considerations of the result of the **SWOT analysis.**

Generic Strategic Planning Approach

Strategic goals, as the **desired state**, elaborate on the **vision**. Once the **current state** is determined, a **gap analysis** is conducted. A **road map** with **milestones** is then developed to bridge the gap, that is, to transit from the current state to the desired state.

A collection of **initiatives** is proposed to make the transition or change with considerations of **constraints**, **resources**, and **risk**. Constraints, assumptions, and resource dependencies can inform risk management; on the other hand, they can be sources of risk and should be managed as risks themselves in some cases.

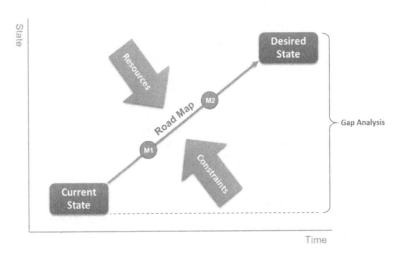

FIGURE 4-7 STRATEGY DEVELOPMENT

Initiatives

An **initiative** is a new attempt or method to achieve a goal or solve a problem. It is typically evaluated by a business analyst, justified by a **business case**, and turned into a **project** by a **sponsor**. **Projects** in a strategy are grouped into **programs** and **portfolios** for synergy.

- A **portfolio** is "a collection of projects, programs, subsidiary portfolios, and operations managed as a group to achieve strategic objectives." (PMI, 2017)

- A **program** is a collection of "related projects, subsidiary programs, and program activities managed in a coordinated manner to obtain benefits not available from managing them individually." (PMI, 2017)

- A **project** is "a temporary endeavor undertaken to create a unique product, service, or result." (PMI, 2017)

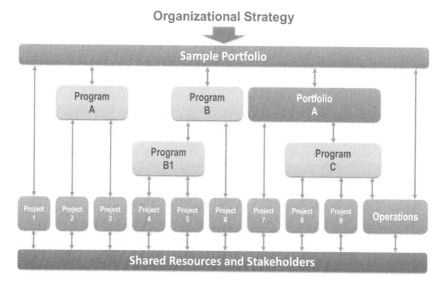

FIGURE 4-8 PORTFOLIOS, PROGRAMS, PROJECTS, OPERATIONS

Action Plan

An action plan is a detailed plan outlining actions needed to reach one or more short-term **objectives** derived from long-term **strategic goals** and organized hierarchically and measured by **key performance indicators (KPIs)** selected from a collection of **metrics and measures**.

<u>2.8.4 Check</u> has details for performance measurement.

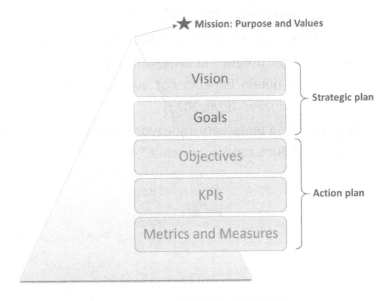

FIGURE 4-9 STRATEGIC AND ACTION PLAN

4.3   STRATEGY EXECUTION

4.3.1   VALUE CREATION PROCESS

Strategy execution implements the strategy to create values, achieve strategic goals, and fulfill organizational vision and mission. A strategy comprises a collection of **initiatives**, usually turned into projects and organized as programs and portfolios. They are carried out to produce various levels of result, such as:

- **Outputs** are the expected deliverable of an initiative.
- **Outcomes** are obtained through the use of outputs.
- **Benefits** are the gains realized by the organization through outputs and outcomes.
- **Value** is the net result of realized benefits less the cost of achieving the benefits.

FIGURE 4-10 VALUE CREATION PROCESS

4.3.2   POLICY DEVELOPMENT

Policies play a crucial role in strategic execution. A policy stands for the "intentions and direction of an organization, as formally expressed by its top management." (ISO 22301) It affects people's behavior and directs an organization's operations.

Depending on the **intention**, some policies are issued to respond to and be compliant with laws or regulations (regulatory policies), while some may be advisory or informative. Besides intention, a policy has a **scope** and may apply to different **audiences or targets** in terms of organizational structure, products or services, geographic locations, information systems, or initiatives, etc.

There are three common types of security-related policies. Program policies are used to create programs. Issue-specific policies address specific issues of concern. System-specific policies focus on the protection of systems.

Policy Type	Examples
Program Policy	• Risk Management Policy • Business Continuity Policy • Incident Response Policy
Issue-specific Policy	• Acceptable Use Policy (AUP) • Access Control Policy • Personnel Security Policy • Physical Security Policy • Secure Application Development Policy • Change Control Policy • E-mail Privacy Policy
System-specific Policy	• Remote Access Policy • Server Security Policy • Router and Switch Security Policy

TABLE 4-2 POLICY TYPES

A policy typically comprises fundamental elements such as objectives, scope, and roles and responsibilities, etc. It can be developed with a top-down or bottom-up approach. Either way, however, has to be approved to proceed; that is, before developing the policy document, approval should be granted to proceed. The policy document shall be approved by the **policy approval authority** to be published and implemented. The policy approval authority is ultimately responsible for subsequent compliance.

Policy Framework

A policy framework refers to the policy and its supporting artifacts, that is, standards, procedures, and guidelines. It is developed to support how the policy is implemented. As policy, standards, procedures, guidelines are closely linked, they may be mixed and published as manuals, handbooks, or similar documents.

Artifact	Usage
Policy	A policy is a statement of the management intent which documents objectives, rules, practices, or regulations, directs the activities, and affects the behavior of people.
Standard	A standard specifies uniform use of specific technologies, parameters, or configurations. For example, a policy may mandate that all devices must be adequately protected. A standard supporting this policy requires all operating systems on PCs must be Windows 10 or higher with a firewall enabled.
Procedure	A procedure is step-by-step instructions to complete a task or activity. E.g., the procedure to install or upgrade Windows 8.
Guideline	A guideline is an **optional** supplement to the policy, standard, or procedure.

TABLE 4-3 POLICY FRAMEWORK

4.3.3   STRATEGY EXECUTION FRAMEWORK

There are many strategy execution frameworks available, such as the 8 model, the INVEST model, the PMI OPM, and so forth. This book introduces the PMI OPM strategy execution framework.

The PMI OPM

The Project Management Institute (PMI) is the United States-based global nonprofit professional organization for project management founded in 1969.

The PMI Organizational Project Management (OPM) is "a **strategy execution framework** utilizing **project**, **program**, and **portfolio** management as well as organizational enabling practices to consistently and predictably deliver organizational strategy producing better performance, better results, and sustainable competitive advantage."

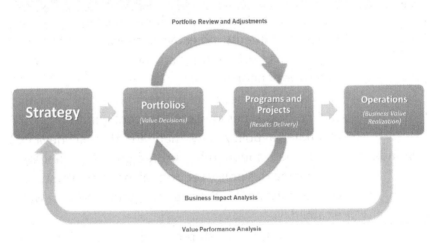

FIGURE 4-11 THE PMI OPM

4.3.4 PROJECT MANAGEMENT

According to the PMI Lexicon of Project Management Terms, a **project** is a temporary endeavor undertaken to create a unique product, service, or result.

Project Management is the application of knowledge, skills, tools, and techniques to project activities to meet the project requirements.

Project Life Cycle

A project has a **life cycle**. It passes through a series of **phases** from its start to its completion. Each phase entails a couple of project management processes that are grouped into project management process groups (Initiating, Planning, Executing Monitoring and Controlling, and Closing).

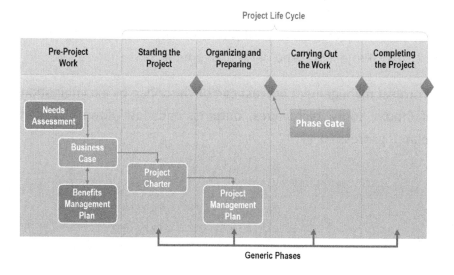

FIGURE 4-12 PROJECT LIFE CYCLE

PMBOK

The Project Management Body of Knowledge (PMBOK) is a set of standard terminology and guidelines for project management published by PMI.

The PMBOK introduces 49 project management processes that fall into five primary project management process groups and ten knowledge areas as follows:

1. Project Integration Management
2. Project Scope Management
3. Project Schedule Management
4. Project Cost Management
5. Project Quality Management
6. Project Resource Management
7. Project Communications Management
8. Project Risk Management
9. Project Procurement Management
10. Project Stakeholder Management

A project management process can be described by a combination of inputs, tools, techniques, outputs, and data flows between related processes.

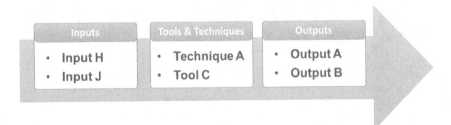

Inputs	Tools & Techniques	Outputs
• Input H • Input J	• Technique A • Tool C	• Output A • Output B

FIGURE 4-13 EXAMPLE PROCESS

Business Case

An initiative should be evaluated through needs analysis and feasibility study and justified by a **business case** with **cost/benefit analysis.**

A business case is a documented economic feasibility study used as a basis for the authorization of further project management activities. A business case can be prepared at the project, program, and portfolio level. It should be traced and managed across the business case life cycle, as the following diagram denotes. (BC: Business Case, HLBC: High-Level Business Case)

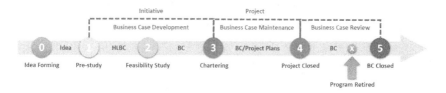

FIGURE 4-14 BUSINESS CASE LIFE CYCLE

Project Charter

A charter is a written constitution or description of an organization's functions. (Google Dictionary) The project charter is a document issued by the project initiator or sponsor that formally authorizes the existence of a project and provides the project manager with authority to apply organizational resources to project activities. When the project charter is approved, the project is formally authorized.

The project charter typically incorporates information about the project's objectives and how it aligns with the organization's strategic goals identified in the business case and ensures a common understanding by the stakeholders of the key deliverables, milestones, and the roles and responsibilities.

Projects are initiated by an entity external to the project. The project initiator or sponsor should be at a level that is appropriate to procure funding and commit resources to the project.

Portfolio, program, and project all need a charter issued by a sponsor or authorized representative for authorization.

- The portfolio charter is a document issued by a sponsor that authorizes and specifies the portfolio structure and links the portfolio to the organization's strategic objectives.
- The program charter is a document issued by a sponsor that authorizes the program management team to use organizational resources to execute the program and links the program to the organization's strategic objectives.

Project Success

A successful project traditionally centers on producing the agreed deliverables on time and on budget, or the triple constraints of scope, time, and cost. Risk, quality, and resources are commonly defined as success factors of a project nowadays.

If the scope, time, or cost are baselined, applying changes to them requires change requests, which follow the change management process.

FIGURE 4-15 PROJECT MANAGEMENT TRIANGLE

Roles and Responsibilities

There are various roles in a project, such as executive management, business analysis, project sponsor, project management office (PMO), project manager, project team member, functional manager, customer/user, vendor, business partner, external stakeholder, and so forth.

The following table introduces three typical project roles and responsibilities:

Role	Responsibilities
Business Analyst	• Determine problems and identify needs • Identify and recommend viable solutions • Elicit, document, and manage requirements • Assist in defining the project • Facilitate project implementation
Project Sponsor	• Issue the project charter • Authorize the project • Assign the project manager • Approve the project management plan • Ensure availability of resources • Make key business decisions for the project • Communicate the project's goals throughout the organization
Project Manager	• Develop the project management plan • Organize and motivate a project team • Manage the scope and deliverables • Manage the schedule • Manage the budget • Manage issues and risk • Monitor progress • Report and communicate

TABLE 4-4 COMMON PROJECT ROLES AND RESPONSIBILITIES

RACI

The RACI model is a popular tool used for identifying roles and responsibilities in a project.

Role/Task	Description
Responsible	Those who do the work to achieve the task are responsible. Responsibility can be shared means that people can collaborate to get the work done.
Accountable	The person is accountable who has the authority to make the final decision and is liable for its result. The person held accountable assigns tasks to project team members responsible for completing the tasks. Accountability should be traceable to one and only one person. In other words, it should not be shared; a board or committee shares and hinders accountability.
Consulted	This role refers to people, typically subject matter experts, consulted for information about making decisions or conducting tasks.
Informed	People affected by project tasks need to be informed of progress and kept up-to-date.

TABLE 4-5 RACI MODEL

The following diagram is an example application of the RACI model:

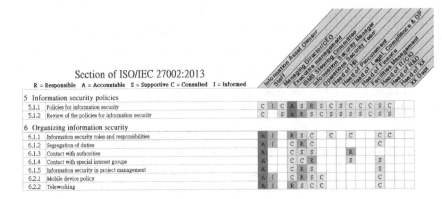

FIGURE 4-16 RACI MATRIX

4.3.5 CHANGE MANAGEMENT

Change management is the process of planning, **controlling**, and monitoring changes to baselines to address risk. **Change control** is part of change management activities.

- **Change** is a controlled modification to a baseline.
- **Baseline** is an approved and formally controlled set of configuration items.
- **Configuration item** can be any type of artifacts, such as hardware, software, or security configuration, requirement, document, scope, cost, schedule, or performance measurement.
- **Configuration** refers to the particular arrangement or pattern of a group of related things.

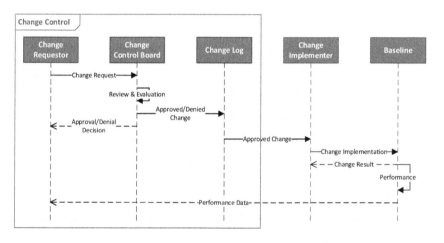

FIGURE 4-17 CHANGE MANAGEMENT

Modification to a baseline requires a **change request**, a formal proposal which should include implementation strategy, costs/benefits analysis, and security implications. Corrective action, preventive action, and defect repairs are common sources of change requests.

The project manager, project sponsor, change control board (CCB), or other authority, as defined in the change management plan, is responsible for reviewing, evaluating, approving or rejecting the change request, and recording it in the change log. Implementation performance is monitored and communicated to stakeholders after the approved change is implemented.

Organizational Change Management

Some define **change** as a move from the current state to the desired state, especially from the strategic perspective of organizational change or transformation. As a result, change is breaking the status quo or changing the state to a better future.

In light of organizational change, successful change management requires changes to behaviors, so there is a significant focus on people, culture, and behaviors.

Change Management and Change Control

However, this book defines management as a structural or systematic approach (e.g., PDCA) to achieve goals or objectives. It distinguishes change management and change control from the perspective of parts and the whole instead of organizational levels or hierarchy.

- **Change Management** is the structural or systematic approach to prevent baselines from creeping or uncontrolled modifications to address risk.
- **Change Control** is part of change management in terms of the PDCA cycle.

Configuration Management

Configuration management aims to manage the composition of configuration items, while change management focuses on the processes and records of changes to baselines.

For example, **configuration management**, in the context of IT or cybersecurity, manages a computer's hardware configurations and informs the system administrator of the details; **change management** controls the changes to the computer, maintains the change log, and monitors and communicates the performance.

The Windows Device Manager manages the hardware configurations, as the following diagram shows. Replacing or upgrading hard drives is a change to the hardware configurations that should be managed by change management.

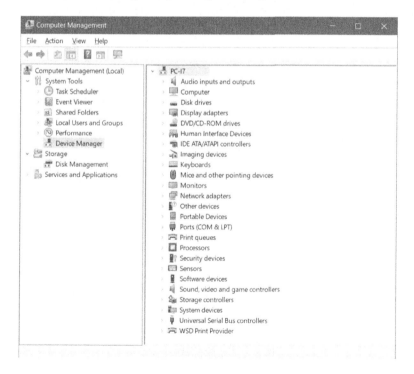

FIGURE 4-18 HARDWARE CONFIGURATIONS

Baselines and Organizational Standards

A baseline is an instance that is compliant with the organizational standard and evolves with changes. An organizational standard typically varies less often than a baseline.

For example, a standard requires all PCs shall be Windows 8 or higher. A snapshot of PCs with Windows 8 is taken as the **configuration baseline**. Let's label it as baseline version 1.0.

As time goes by, a change request to upgrade the PCs to Windows 8.1 is submitted. It is approved and implemented; the baseline version 1.0 is shifted to baseline version 1.1, Windows 8.1.

As we all know, the latest baseline is version 1.1 (Windows 8.1), while the standard remains intact, Windows 8 or higher.

4.3.6   SECURITY OPERATIONS

Definition

> ***Security operations***, *as part of business operations, entails ongoing day-to-day execution of security activities per the standards, procedures, and guidelines to enforce the security policy and support business operations.*

Business operations are ongoing activities that produce long-term, repetitive outputs, such as manufacturing products or supplying services.

Operations management is concerned with producing goods and delivering services to meet customer demands by using the optimal resources needed.

Projects vs. Security Operations

The Project Management Institute (PMI) defines a **project** as a temporary endeavor undertaken to create a unique product, service, or result. Unlike a project as a temporary endeavor, **security operations** are ongoing execution of security activities.

A project is closed after its results are delivered and turned into operations. For example, a one-year project is initiated for the initial certification of ISO 27001. The project is closed after the ISMS gets certified. However, the practice of ISMS that has been put into operations is an ongoing activity.

Security Operations Activities

Typical security operations include but not limited to the following activities:

1. Regular Tasks
   a. Securely provisioning resources
   b. Implement recovery strategies
   c. Configuration management
   d. Change management
2. Security Operation Center (SOC)
   a. Conduct logging and monitoring activities
   b. Operate and maintain detective and preventative measures
   c. Conduct incident management
   d. Support investigations
3. Security Assessment
   a. Vulnerability management
   b. Continuous Monitoring
4. Business Continuity
   a. Participate in Business Continuity (BC) planning and exercises
   b. Implement Disaster Recovery (DR) processes
   c. Test Disaster Recovery Plans (DRP)

REVIEW QUESTIONS

1. **To which of the following levels of strategy does cost leadership belong?**
   A. Corporate strategy
   B. Business strategy
   C. Functional strategy
   D. Tactic

2. **Which of the following refers to strategies at a lower level should be aligned with those at the upper level?**
   A. Strategic alignment
   B. Strategic thinking
   C. Strategic formulation
   D. Strategic implementation

3. **Which of the following states the organization's purpose and values?**
   A. Action plan
   B. Mission statement
   C. Policy
   D. Strategic plan

4. **The SWOT analysis identifies all of the following except:**
   A. Organization's weaknesses
   B. Organization's strengths
   C. Opportunities and threats
   D. Action plans

5. **Which of the following is the essential component of strategic portfolios?**
   A. Tactics
   B. Action plan
   C. Project
   D. Policy

6. **Which of the following refers to the intentions and direction of an organization, as formally expressed by its top management?**
   A. Vision
   B. Strategy
   C. Policy
   D. Mission

7. **Which of the following should be initiated and chartered to implement a strategy?**
   A. Operations
   B. Policy
   C. Program
   D. Vision

8. **Which of the following can be baselined in a project?**
   A. Scope
   B. Schedule
   C. Cost
   D. All of the above

9. **Which of the following is not true about change management (CM)?**
   A. CM is not required if the configuration is not baselined.
   B. A change request is required.
   C. Only approved change requests can be implemented.
   D. Change requests should always be approved.

10. **Which of the following is not part of security operations?**
    A. Incident response
    B. Change management
    C. Strategic planning
    D. Continuous monitoring

5 INFORMATION SECURITY RISK MANAGEMENT

"It's in vain to talk about risk without objectives in mind."

- Wentz Wu

5.1   WHAT IS INFORMATION SECURITY RISK?

The definition of **information security risk** or **information risk** is derived from ISO 31000 and the NIST generic risk model as follows:

Definition

> **Information security risk** *is the risk that a threat source* **might** *initiate threat events to exploit vulnerabilities, which would cause an adverse* **impact** *on the confidentiality, integrity, and availability of information assets.*

Information Security Risk Management

Information security risk management is the management of risk to ensure **information security**, which aims to protect information assets from threats through safeguards to achieve the objectives of confidentiality, integrity, and availability, support business, and create and deliver values.

Risk Management Frameworks

ISO 31000 (general risk concepts), COSO ERM (organization tier), and PMI RMP (project-level risk) have been introduced in 3.4 Risk Management. This chapter focuses on information risk and related frameworks such as ISO 27005 and NIST FARM.

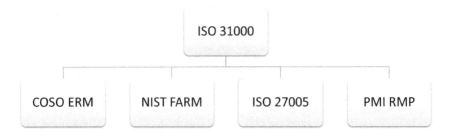

FIGURE 3-6 ENTERPRISE ARCHITECTURE FRAMEWORKS

5.2 ISO 27005

ISO 27005 provides guidelines for **information security risk management**. It supports the implementation of ISO 27001, demonstrates legal compliance and evidence of due diligence, prepares for a business continuity plan (BCP) or incident response plan (IRP), or describes the information security requirements for a product, a service or a mechanism.

ISO 27000 Series of Standards

- ISO/IEC 27000, Information technology — Security techniques — Information security management systems — Overview and vocabulary
- ISO/IEC 27001, Information technology — Security techniques — Information security management systems — Requirements
- ISO/IEC 27002, Information technology — Security techniques — Code of practice for information security controls
- ISO/IEC 27005, Information technology — Security techniques — Information security risk management
- ISO/IEC 27701, Security techniques — Extension to ISO/IEC 27001 and ISO/IEC 27002 for privacy information management — Requirements and guidelines

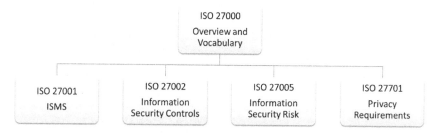

FIGURE 5-1 ISO 27000 SERIES

Information Security Risk Management Process

The information security risk management process is derived from ISO 31000, as the following diagram shows:

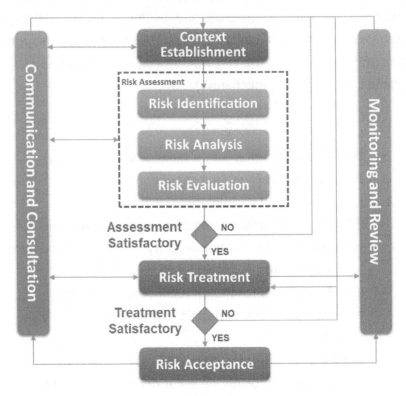

FIGURE 5-2 ISO 27005

5.2.1   CONTEXT ESTABLISHMENT

To establish the context means to analyze and understand the organization and its context (external and internal context), and stakeholders to determine basic criteria, the scope and boundaries, and the organization for information security risk management (roles and responsibilities), etc.

The external and internal context for information security risk management is the environment where the organization and its stakeholders interact with one another, which affects risk management decisions and activities.

Basic Criteria

ISO 27005 provides guidelines for the establishment of the Information Security risk management approach. An appropriate risk management approach should be selected or developed that addresses basic criteria such as risk evaluation criteria, impact criteria, risk acceptance criteria.

Scope and Boundaries

Defining the scope starts with the study of the organization to understand how information and information systems get involved in supporting the organization's operations, strategies, vision, and mission.

The defined scope ensures that all relevant assets are taken into account in the risk assessment. Examples of the risk management scope may be an IT application, IT infrastructure, a business process, or a defined part of an organization.

There are two types of assets: primary and supporting assets. Supporting assets are assets on which the primary assets of the scope rely. Primary assets include business processes and activities and information. Hardware, software, network, personnel, site, and organization's structure are supporting assets.

Risk Management Organization

The organization, roles, and responsibilities for the information security risk management process should be set up and maintained.

5.2.2   RISK ASSESSMENT

Risk assessment consists of three activities: risk identification, risk analysis, and risk evaluation. It determines the value of the information assets, identifies the applicable threats, vulnerabilities, and the existing controls, determines the likelihood and consequences of risks, and prioritizes the risks against the risk evaluation criteria set in the context establishment.

Risk assessment is often conducted in two (or more) iterations: high-level and detailed assessment.

- The high-level risk assessment concentrates more on the business and operational environment than technological elements. It focuses on attack scenarios rather than their elements, uses risk domains or categories instead of individual risks, and prefers common to specific controls.
- The detailed risk assessment process involves an in-depth assessment of assets, threats, and vulnerabilities. The results of the assessment are then used to identify risk treatment. It is usually most suitable for information systems at high risk because it requires considerable time, effort, and expertise and can be.

It is up to the organization to select its own approach to risk assessment based on the objectives and the aim of the risk assessment.

5.2.3 RISK IDENTIFICATION

Risk identification involves the following activities, which can be conducted in a different order depending on the methodology applied.

1. Identification of assets
2. Identification of threats
3. Identification of existing controls
4. Identification of vulnerabilities
5. Identification of consequences

Vulnerability is the "weakness of an asset or control that can be exploited by one or more threats."

The threat is "potential cause of an unwanted incident, which can result in harm to a system or organization."

5.2.4 RISK ANALYSIS

Risk analysis assigns values to the **likelihood** and **consequences** of risk against a scale of either **qualitative attributes** or **quantitative numbers**, determines the **level of risk**, and generates a list of estimated risks which serves as the input of risk evaluation. The form of risk analysis should be consistent with the risk evaluation criteria developed as part of establishing the context.

Assessment of consequences is conducted in terms of business impact because of loss or compromise of assets. The consequences or business impact is determined by three factors: the **criticality**, **replacement cost**, and related **business loss**. Business impact analysis (BIA) determines the business impact by taking into account these three factors. Criticality, the basis of asset classification and BIA, is the importance of fulfilling the business objectives of the organization.

In summary, the assessment of consequences or business impact determined using two measures:

- The replacement cost of assets
- Business loss because of loss or compromise of assets evaluated based on their criticality

The output of risk analysis is a list of risks with value levels assigned based on assessed consequences and the likelihood of incident scenarios.

The following is a sample output of risk analysis:

Risk	Consequence	Likelihood	Risk Score	Ranking
Risk A	5	2	10	
Risk B	2	4	8	
Risk C	4	5	20	
Risk D	3	3	9	
Risk E	4	1	4	
Risk F	2	4	8	

TABLE 5-1 SAMPLE RISK ANALYSIS OUTPUT

5.2.5   RISK EVALUATION

Risk evaluation is the process of prioritizing risk and deciding whether actions should be taken as risk treatment by comparing the level of risks against risk evaluation criteria and risk acceptance criteria resulted from the outcome of risk analysis. The output of risk evaluation is a list of risks prioritized according to risk evaluation criteria in relation to the incident scenarios that lead to those risks.

Given a sample risk evaluation and acceptance criteria as follows:

Risk Evaluation Criteria	Risk Acceptance Criteria
• Risk Score • The criticality of assets • Stakeholder's expectations	A risk score that is less than 6

TABLE 5-2 RISK EVALUATION AND ACCEPTANCE CRITERIA

The following is a sample risk evaluation output:

Risk	Consequence	Likelihood	Risk Score	Ranking
Risk C	4	5	20	1
Risk A	5	2	10	2
Risk D	3	3	9	3
Risk F	2	4	8	4
Risk B	2	4	8	5
Risk E	4	1	4	6

TABLE 5-3 SAMPLE RISK EVALUATION OUTPUT

Risk E is accepted as its risk score is less than 6. Other risks are prioritized based on the risk evaluation criteria.

5.2.6   RISK TREATMENT

Risk treatment is the process of selecting **risk treatment options** and determining **controls**, if needed, to reduce, retain, avoid, or share the risks to define a **risk treatment plan**. The outcome of **risk assessment** and **cost/benefit analysis** are significant factors when developing a risk treatment plan, which should identify the **priority** and **timeframes** for individual risk treatments.

There are four typical options available for risk treatment: **risk modification, risk retention, risk avoidance,** and **risk sharing**. They either change the likelihood or consequences of risk. They are not mutually exclusive, and multiple options can be applied as a combination.

Managers should also consider **rare but severe risks** that may not be justifiable from a strictly economic perspective. For example, business continuity controls covering specific high risks may not be justified in terms of economic return.

Residual risks need to be determined by another iteration of the risk assessment conducted when the risk treatment plan has been defined. Further risk assessments that take into account the expected effects of the planned risk treatment should be conducted iteratively until the residual risk meets the organization's risk acceptance criteria.

Risk Modification

The risk treatment option, risk modification, identifies a list of possible controls with cost, benefit, and priority. It modifies either the likelihood, consequences, or both to manage the level of risk by introducing, removing, or altering **controls** so that the reassessed **residual risk** can be accepted.

Controls provide various types of protection, such as correction, elimination, prevention, impact minimization, deterrence, detection, recovery, monitoring, and awareness. ISO/IEC 27002 supplements detailed information on controls. The selection of controls should take into account the **cost/benefit** and **specialized skills** needed to define and implement new controls or modify existing ones.

Constraints that can affect the selection or implementation of controls should also be considered, for example, financial constraints, technical constraints, operational constraints, cultural constraints, ethical constraints, environmental constraints, ease of use, personnel constraints, constraints for integrating new and existing controls.

Risk Retention

No, or no more, treatment is one treatment. Risk retention is the decision to retain the risk without further action based on the outcome of risk evaluation. The risk can be retained if the level of risk meets the risk acceptance criteria. That is, there is no need to implement additional controls.

Risk Avoidance

Risk avoidance is the decision to give up the activity or condition that gives rise to a particular risk. This decision is made when the identified risks are considered too high, or other risk treatment options are cost-ineffective (the costs exceed the benefits).

For example, Because of being subject to the risk of data integrity and availability, some global cloud service providers give up building data centers in regions where power supply is unstable. Giving up building data centers or relocating to other regions with stable utility is risk avoidance.

Risk Sharing

Risk sharing is the decision to share certain risks with other parties. However, only the responsibility of conducting activities that may give rise to the risk and managing the risk is shared instead of the **liability** of an impact. Additional risk treatment can be necessary, as risk sharing can create new risks or modify existing, identified risks. **Insurance** that covers the consequences or **outsourcing** work to a partner is good examples of risk sharing.

5.2.7   RISK ACCEPTANCE

Risk acceptance and risk retention may be used interchangeably in other risk management frameworks. However, there are some minute differences from the perspective of ISO 27005.

- **Risk retention** is the risk treatment option that no action is taken given the inherent or residual risk meets the risk acceptance criteria defined when establishing the risk context.
- In contrast, **risk acceptance** is a decision on whether the residual risk, produced after risk treatments, such as risk modification, risk share, or risk avoidance, is explicitly accepted by the managers.

For those accepted risks that do not meet the normal risk acceptance criteria, the outcome of risk acceptance should highlight them with stated justification. Risk acceptance criteria may become inadequate and should be revised, but it is not always possible to do so promptly.

For example, when it comes to accepting risk with desirable benefits or high cost of risk modification, odds are the outdated risk acceptance criteria cannot be revised timely. In this situation, the decision-maker should explicitly comment on the risks and include a justification for the decision to override normal risk acceptance criteria.

5.3   NIST FARM

NIST FRAM refers to the risk management approach introduced in the NIST guideline, National Institute of Standards and Technology (NIST) Special Publication SP 800-39. It is intended to be a complement to and should be used as part of a more comprehensive Enterprise Risk Management (ERM) program.

This guideline addresses the management of information security-related risk derived from or associated with the operation and use of information systems or the environments in which those systems operate.

NIST FARM Suggested Readings

The following are suggested readings for NIST FARM:

1. NIST SP 800-39, Managing Information Security Risk: Organization, Mission, and Information System View, March 2011.
2. NIST SP 800-30, Revision 1, Guide for Conducting Risk Assessments, September 2012.
3. NIST SP 800-37, Revision 2, Guide for Applying the Risk Management Framework to Federal Information Systems: A Security Life Cycle Approach, December 2018.
4. NIST SP 800-137, Information Security Continuous Monitoring for Federal Information Systems and Organizations, September 2011.
5. NIST SP 800-160, Volume 1, Systems Security Engineering: Considerations for a Multidisciplinary Approach in the Engineering of Trustworthy Secure Systems, November 2016.

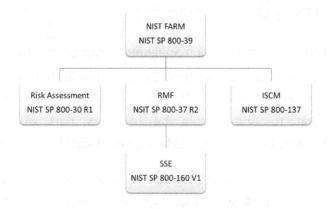

FIGURE 5-3 NIST FARM SUGGESTED READINGS

- NIST SP 800-39 introduces the **FARM** (Frame, Assess, Respond, Monitor) framework.

- NIST SP 800-30 R1 and NIST SP 800-137 deal with the **Assess** and **Monitor** components, respectively.

- It is worthy of noticing that NIST SP 800-37 R2 primarily deals with security at the tier of information systems, as the following diagram shows.

- NIST SP 800-160 V1 addresses security in terms of the system development life cycle (SDLC). It has superseded NIST SP 800-64 R2.

FIGURE 5-4 RISK MANAGEMENT FRAMEWORK

NIST FARM Components

NIST FARM is an integrated, organization-wide risk management approach. It comprises four components: Frame, Assess, Respond, and Monitor (FARM) and includes the following considerations:

- Strategic goals and objectives
- Missions and business functions
- Mission and business processes
- Enterprise and information security architectures
- System development life cycle (SDLC) processes

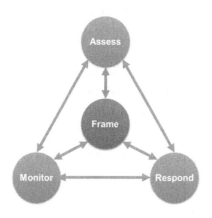

FIGURE 5-5 NIST FARM

Multi-Tiered Risk Management

NIST FARM deals with risk in terms of three tiers: **organization**, **mission/business processes**, and **information systems**.

According to the Continuity Guidance Circular 2 (CGC 2) of the Federal Emergency Management Agency (FEMA), a **mission** typically is something unique the organization does. Organizations generally conduct different types of **mission functions** supported by a variety of **business processes** that are supported by **information systems** to achieve organizational objectives.

Organizational objectives are broken down to lower levels or tiers, each of which is associated with risk that may hinder the pursuit of objectives.

The following are common risks at different tiers:

- Tier 1: failing to comply with legal or regulatory requirements, damaging reputation or relationships, causing financial loss, or undermining long-term viability.
- Tier 2: failing to fully meet mission/business objectives or successfully execute a specific mission/business process.
- Tier 3: failing to perform required functions of information systems or losing confidentiality, integrity, or availability.

NIST FARM components apply to all the three tiers of the organization. However, the **Frame** component is primarily conducted at the **organization** tier. Its primary output is the risk management strategy that directs activities in the other three components (Assess, Respond, and Monitor).

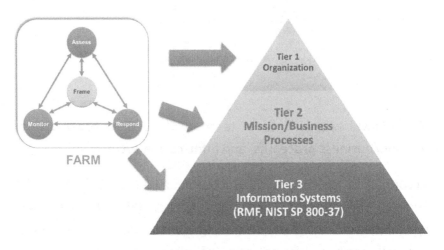

FIGURE 5-6 MULTI-TIERED RISK MANAGEMENT

The following table is an excerpt from NIST SP 800-39.

Task	Task Description
Step 1: Risk Framing	
TASK 1-1 Risk Assumptions	Identify assumptions that affect how risk is assessed, responded to, and monitored within the organization.
TASK 1-2 Risk Constraints	Identify constraints on the conduct of risk assessment, risk response, and risk monitoring activities within the organization.
TASK 1-3 Risk Tolerance	Identify the level of risk tolerance for the organization.
TASK 1-4 Priorities and Trade-offs	Identify priorities and trade-offs considered by the organization in managing risk.
Step 2: Risk Assessment	
TASK 2-1 Threat and Vulnerability Identification	Identify threats to and vulnerabilities in organizational information systems and the environments in which the systems operate.
TASK 2-2 Risk Determination	Determine the risk to organizational operations and assets, individuals, other organizations, and the Nation if identified threats exploit identified vulnerabilities.
Step 3: Risk Response	
TASK 3-1 Risk Response Identification	Identify alternative courses of action to respond to risk determined during the risk assessment.
TASK 3-2 Evaluation of Alternatives	Evaluate alternative courses of action for responding to risk.
TASK 3-3 Risk Response Decision	Decide on the appropriate course of action for responding to risk.
TASK 3-4 Risk Response Implementation	Implement the course of action selected to respond to risk.
Step 4: Risk Monitoring	
TASK 4-1 Risk Monitoring Strategy	Develop a risk monitoring strategy for the organization that includes the purpose, type, and frequency of monitoring activities.
TASK 4-2 Risk Monitoring	Monitor organizational information systems and environments of operation on an ongoing basis to verify compliance, determine effectiveness of risk response measures, and identify changes.

FIGURE 5-7 NIST FARM PROCESS TASKS

5.3.1 FRAME

The first component of risk management is "Frame" or risk framing. Its purpose is to establish the **risk context** for all three tiers (organization, mission/business processes, and information systems) and develop a **risk management strategy** that directs the risk management process (assess, respond, and monitor).

To frame risk or risk framing means to establish a risk context or risk frame. More specifically, it describes the environment in which risk-based decisions are made. Risk framing collects **information** from a variety of sources as inputs to form the risk context, such as 1) organizational governance structure, 2) financial posture, 3) legal/regulatory environment, 4) investment strategy, 5) culture, and 6) trust relationships established within and among organizations.

FIGURE 5-8 RISK FRAMING

The risk framing step also produces a set of organizational policies, procedures, standards, guidance, and resources to implement the risk management strategy.

Investment Strategies

Investment strategies reflect the long-term strategic goals and objectives of organizations, and risk management strategies ensure success. In order to enforce information security, investment strategies should consider the following issues:

- Replacing **legacy** information systems
- Outsourcing and using **external** providers
- Internal development or external acquisition decisions

Trust Relationship

Trust relationships are critical factors in risk decisions, as organizations increasingly rely on external providers and partnerships. This reliance results in the needs for trust relationships among organizations. Trustworthiness plays a crucial role in establishing trust relationships among persons and organizations.

Organizations can obtain the levels of trust needed to form partnerships through trust models, such as 1) validated rust, 2) direct historical trust, 3) mediated trust, 4) mandated trust, and 5) hybrid trust model. 0 Procurement and Supply Chain has details.

Trust is a belief that an entity will behave in a predictable manner in specified circumstances.

Trustworthiness is an attribute of a person, organization, product, or system that provides confidence to others in terms of qualifications, capabilities, and reliability.

Risk Management Strategy

The risk management strategy is then developed as part of the risk context, also known as risk frame, which consists of 1) risk assumptions, 2) risk constraints, 3) risk tolerance, 4) priorities and trade-offs, and 5) guidance to assess risk, respond to risk, and monitor risk, such as **risk assessment methodologies**, risk response strategies, a process for evaluating risk, and approaches for monitoring risk.

FIGURE 5-9 RISK MANAGEMENT STRATEGY

Risk Tolerance

Risk tolerance is the level of risk or degree of uncertainty that is acceptable to organizations and is a crucial element of the organizational risk frame.

It is crucial that organizations exercise due diligence in determining risk tolerance - recognizing how fundamental this decision is to the effectiveness of the risk management program.

Guidance

Risk assessments are guided by the **risk assessment methodologies** determined in the risk management strategy developed during the **risk framing** step of the risk management process.

A risk management strategy should also provide guidance to risk response and monitoring.

5.3.2 ASSESS

The second component of risk management is "Access." Risk assessments can be conducted at all three tiers - organization, mission/business processes, and information systems.

Its purpose is to determine the risk level in terms of the likelihood, impact, and other risk factors and supports risk-based decisions and activities.

Risk Assessment Methodologies

A **risk assessment methodology** typically includes 1) risk model, 2) analysis approach, 3) assessment approach, and 4) risk assessment process.

FIGURE 5-10 RISK ASSESSMENT METHODOLOGY

1. A **risk model** defines vital terms and assessable risk factors and the relationships among the factors, as Figure 2-10 NIST Generic Risk Model shows.
2. An **analysis approach** describes how combinations of risk factors are identified and analyzed, such as **threat-oriented**, **asset/impact-oriented**, or **vulnerability-oriented** approach; they are approaches used to identify risk in terms of the risk model.

3. An **assessment approach** determines or specifies values against a scale to risk factors (e.g., likelihood or impact) so that the combined values of risk factors in the risk model can be used to evaluate risk. Assessment approaches can be **quantitative, qualitative**, or **semi-qualitative**.

4. A **risk assessment process** typically comprises the following steps. The **identification** procedure in "Step 2: Conduct Assessment" may vary depending on the **analysis** approach.

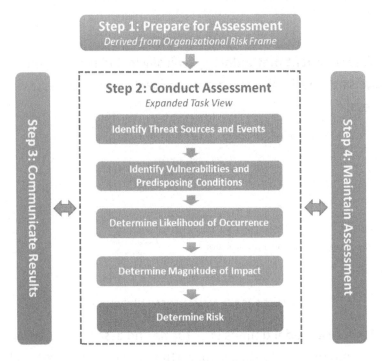

FIGURE 5-11 RISK ASSESSMENT PROCESS

Confusing Terminologies

The terms "**analysis approach**" and "**assessment approach**" in the methodology of "**risk assessment**" may be confusing to many people because, in ISO 27005 and ISO 31000, risk assessment is a wrapper process that comprises 1) risk identification, 2) risk analysis, and 3) risk evaluation as shown in Figure 5-2 ISO 27005.

In NIST FARM, the "analysis approach" is used to "identify risk" from different orientations, while the "assessment approach" is employed to "analyze risk" compared with ISO.

When we say, "we are conducting a risk assessment," are we referring to the wrapper process of risk assessment or the sub-process of analyzing risk to determine the likelihood or impact? As a result, it is not specific enough for the CISSP Exam Outline to state the topic with the wording, "Risk Assessment/Analysis."

NIST Risk "Analysis Approach"

There are three approaches used to identify risk: **threat-oriented**, **asset/impact-oriented**, or **vulnerability-oriented** approach.

Organizations can choose a particular analysis approach according to their requirements. For example, when conducting the risk assessment at Tier 2, a Business Impact Analysis (BIA) typically focuses on identifying critical business process (primary assets) and dependent supporting resources, and adverse impacts first. It is an example of an **asset/impact-oriented** analysis approach. For further information about BIA, please refer to the following sources:

- DHS Federal Continuity Directive 2 (FCD-2) provides guidance on BIAs at the organization and mission/business process level.
- NIST SP 800-34 R1 provides guidance on BIAs at the information system level.

A **threat scenario** is a combination of a threat source and a threat event. As one threat source may initiate multiple threat events, and one threat event can be initiated by multiple threat sources, it shapes a **many-to-many** relationship.

The **threat-oriented analysis** may involve complicated and large amounts of threat scenarios. Thanks to automated modeling and simulation and graph-based analysis techniques, large numbers of threat scenarios can be restricted to a reasonable subset of all possible threat scenarios.

Functional dependency network analysis, attack tree analysis for adversarial threats, fault tree analysis for other types of threats are conventional graph-based analysis techniques.

NIST Risk "Assessment Approach"

The NIST "assessment approach" is used to assign values to risk factors defined in the risk model. Likelihood and consequences are two of the most significant risk factors. There are three types of risk assessment approach: **qualitative**, **quantitative**, and **semi-quantitative**. As most of the risk management frameworks use two types of approaches: qualitative and quantitative, it is not uncommon for people to treat a semi-quantitative approach as a quantitative approach.

A risk might cause a financial loss of $5,000,000 calculated by the quantitative approach. It can be classified as a "high" impact risk based on experience using a qualitative approach.

Qualitative	Semi-Quantitative		Quantitative
	Bins	Scales	
Very High	96-100	5	>= $10,000,000
High	80-95	4	< $10,000,000
Moderate	21-79	3	< $1,000,000
Low	5-20	2	< $100,000
Very Low	0-4	1	< $10,000

TABLE 5-4 SAMPLE ASSESSMENT VALUES

Qualitative Approach

Qualitative approach primarily collects unstructured data and relies on subjective perception, experience, judgment, or intuition. A qualitative approach, for example, would use a scale of "Low, Medium, High" to indicate the likelihood or impact of a risk event occurring.

Quantitative Approach

The quantitative approach typically collects structured data and numbers and employs statistical techniques, such as time-series analysis, regression analysis, or simulation. It is more objective than the qualitative approach. For example, the estimated financial loss by regression analysis can be as high as $552,000.

Semi-quantitative Approach

The third type of risk analysis is called semi-quantitative analysis that can provide the benefits of quantitative and qualitative analysis.

Values like **qualitative labels** (Low/High), **bins** (e.g., 0-4, 5-20, 21-79, 80-95, 96-100) or **scales** (e.g., 1-5) can be translated or mapped to one another. It helps decision-makers understand and compare them, e.g., a score of 95 can be interpreted as very high; risks scored 70, and 71 respectively make no significant difference; the risks scored 70 cause more adverse impact that a risk scored 30.

Summary of Risk Assessment Tasks

The following table is an excerpt from NIST SP 800-30 R1:

Task	Task Description
Step 1: Prepare for Risk Assessment	
TASK 1-1 Identify Purpose	Identify the purpose of the risk assessment in terms of the information that the assessment is intended to produce and the decisions the assessment is intended to support.
TASK 1-2 Identify Scope	Identify the scope of the risk assessment in terms of organizational applicability, time frame supported, and architectural/technology considerations.
TASK 1-3 Identify Assumptions and Constraints	Identify the specific assumptions and constraints under which the risk assessment is conducted.
TASK 1-4 Identify Information Sources	Identify the sources of descriptive, threat, vulnerability, and impact information to be used in the risk assessment.
TASK 1-5 Identify Risk Model and Analytic Approach	Identify the risk model and analytic approach to be used in the risk assessment.
Step 2: Conduct Risk Assessment	
TASK 2-1 Identify Threat Sources	Identify and characterize threat sources of concern, including capability, intent, and targeting characteristics for adversarial threats and range of effects for non-adversarial threats.
TASK 2-2 Identify Threat Events	Identify potential threat events, relevance of the events, and the threat sources that could initiate the events.
TASK 2-3 Identify Vulnerabilities and Predisposing Conditions	Identify vulnerabilities and predisposing conditions that affect the likelihood that threat events of concern result in adverse impacts.
TASK 2-4 Determine Likelihood	Determine the likelihood that threat events of concern result in adverse impacts, considering: (i) the characteristics of the threat sources that could initiate the events; (ii) the vulnerabilities/predisposing conditions identified; and (iii) the organizational susceptibility reflecting the safeguards or countermeasures planned or implemented to impede such events.

Task	Task Description
TASK 2-5 Determine Impact	Determine the adverse impacts from threat events of concern, considering: (i) the characteristics of the threat sources that could initiate the events; (ii) the vulnerabilities/predisposing conditions identified; and (iii) the organizational susceptibility reflecting the safeguards/countermeasures planned or implemented to impede such events.
TASK 2-6 Determine Risk	Determine the risk to the organization from threat events of concern considering: (i) the impact that would result from the events; and (ii) the likelihood of the events occurring.
Step 3: Communicate and Share Risk Assessment Results	
TASK 3-1 Communicate Risk Assessment Results	Communicate risk assessment results to organizational decision makers to support risk responses.
TASK 3-2 Share Risk-related Information	Share risk-related information produced during the risk assessment with appropriate organizational personnel.
Step 4: Maintain Risk Assessment	
TASK 4-1 Monitor Risk Factors	Conduct ongoing monitoring of the risk factors that contribute to changes in risk to organizational operations and assets, individuals, other organizations, or the Nation.
TASK 4-2 Update Risk Assessment	Update existing risk assessment using the results from ongoing monitoring of risk factors.

TABLE 5-5 SUMMARY OF RISK ASSESSMENT TASKS

5.3.3   RESPOND

The third component of risk management is "Respond." Risk response identifies, evaluates, selects, and implements appropriate **courses of action** with considerations of **risk tolerance** and **cost-benefit**.

A **course of action** is a time-phased or situation-dependent combination of risk response measures or specific actions taken to respond to risk.

Risk response addresses how organizations handle risk once risk is determined through risk assessments. In order to support the risk response, organizations describe common types of **risk response measures** and how the **courses of action** are developed, evaluated, and communicated.

Common types of risk response measures include:

- **Accept** risk if it is tolerable or economically unjustifiable
- **Avoid** risk by giving up doing something
- **Mitigate** risk by reducing the likelihood and/or impact
- **Share** (partly) or **transfer** (wholly) risk to third parties

While each type of risk response measure can have an associated risk response strategy, it is common to develop an **overall risk response strategy** that selects and combines from among the basic risk response types above.

For example, a flood may threaten the data center. Your organization might conduct a site selection survey and implement flood control gates to **mitigate** the risk and buy insurance to **share** the loss of data center or deploy services to the cloud to **transfer** the risk.

It comprises four tasks to develop a risk response strategy:

1. Identify alternative courses of action
2. Evaluate alternative courses of action
3. Select the appropriate course of action
4. Implement the selected course of action

Risk Acceptance

Risk acceptance is appropriate when the identified risk is within the organizational risk tolerance. Organizations may accept any level of risk, no matter it is low, moderate, or high, to respond to particular situations or conditions.

For example, earthquakes are almost unavoidable. Organizations tend to accept the risk that earthquakes might threaten data centers because large earthquakes happen infrequently, and addressing such risk is not cost-effective.

Revisions to information systems shall be verified, validated, certified, and authorized to put into operation. However, the management may accept the risk to authorize a system lacking thorough testing to go online for emergencies, e.g., the system supporting the logistics of medical materials against the novel coronavirus 2019 (Covid19) to save human life.

Risk Avoidance

Risk avoidance may be appropriate when the identified risk exceeds organizational risk tolerance.

Organizations may conduct certain types of activities or employ certain types of information technologies that result in risk that is unacceptable. In such situations, risk avoidance involves taking specific actions to eliminate the activities or technologies that are the basis for the risk or to revise or reposition these activities or technologies in the organizational mission/business processes to avoid the potential for unacceptable risk.

For example, supply chain risk is a significant concern. Giving up 5G solutions from a 5G supplier with an infamous reputation of embedding back doors in their products is an example of risk avoidance.

Giving up interconnections between two information systems or security domains or isolating a network as an "air-gapped" one employing manual data transfer are other examples.

Risk Mitigation

Risk mitigation, or risk reduction, is appropriate if the risk cannot be accepted, avoided, shared, or transferred. It typically reduces the likelihood and/or impact of risk.

Organizations may mitigate risk with a combination of risk response measures across the three tiers. For example, risk mitigation can include common security controls specified at the organizational level (Tier 1), business process reengineering (BPR) at mission/business process level (Tier 2), and new or enhanced security controls or overlays at information systems level (Tier 3).

Risk Sharing or Transfer

Risk sharing and risk transfer reduce neither the likelihood nor the impact of risk. They are appropriate when organizations desire and have the means to shift risk to other organizations.

Risk sharing shifts a portion of the risk to other organizations; risk transfer shifts the entire risk to another organization. Insurance and outsourcing are common means of risk sharing or transfer.

5.3.4 MONITOR

The fourth component of risk management is "Monitor."

After an information system is authorized to operate, the system and the system-specific and common security controls shall be monitored. There are three types of risk monitoring: **compliance, effectiveness,** and **change monitoring**. The purpose of monitoring risk is to:

- Ensure **compliance** that the risk response measures are implemented correctly and operating as intended.
- Determine the **effectiveness** that the implemented risk response measures have been reducing identified risk to the desired level.
- Identify **changes** that may introduce new risks or affect existing ones.

Monitoring risk should be on an ongoing basis, in a timely manner, and with consideration of automated versus manual methods and the frequency of monitoring.

Automated Monitoring

Organizations should maximize the use of automation wherever possible. However, monitoring at Tier 1 (organization) and Tier 2 (mission/business processes) are generally not automated, but it is not uncommon that monitoring at Tier 3 (information systems) adopts automation because of the technical nature.

Automation is particularly useful in the following areas:

- Assessment and **continuous monitoring** of controls
- Preparation of **authorization packages**
- Implementation of **ongoing authorization** approaches

Continuous Monitoring

Monitoring for control effectiveness is a form of control assessment. Continuous monitoring promotes effective and efficient risk management on an ongoing basis. Control assessment and continuous monitoring together facilitate a real-time or near real-time risk-based decision-making process, for example, ongoing authorization.

In other words, **Continuous monitoring** helps to achieve **ongoing authorization,** a state in which security and privacy information for controls are generated and collected at the frequency specified in the organization's continuous monitoring strategy.

The terms "continuous" and "ongoing" here mean that security controls and organizational risks are assessed and analyzed at a frequency sufficient to support risk-based security decisions to protect organization information adequately.

Authorization Packages

Authorization is the process by which a senior management official, the authorizing official, reviews security and privacy information describing the current security and privacy posture of **information systems** or **common controls** that are inherited by systems. (NIST SP 800-37 R2)

- A **type authorization** is an official authorization decision that allows for a single authorization package to be developed for an archetype (i.e., common) version of a system.
- A **facility authorization** is an official authorization decision that is focused on specific controls implemented in a

defined environment of operation to support one or more systems residing within that environment.

The output of system authorization comprises:

- the authorization decision,
- terms and conditions for the authorization,
- time-driven authorization frequency or authorization termination date, and
- events that may trigger a review of the authorization decision (if any).

Appendix F in NIST SP 800-37 R2 (RMF) has more details about authorization.

A system and common control shall be authorized to operate. A system authorization or a common control authorization can be an **initial authorization, ongoing authorization,** or **reauthorization.** The NIST Risk Management Framework (RMF) describes the process for obtaining authorization (Step 5) and monitoring security controls at the system level (Step 6).

The purpose of the authorization to operate (ATO) or authorization to use is to determine if the security and privacy risk are acceptable. In order to get the ATO, an authorization package is developed and submitted to the authorizing official via automated means or manual means. An authorization package includes:

- An executive summary
- Security and privacy plans
- Security and privacy assessment reports
- Plans of action and milestones (POA&M)
- Additional Information at the request of the authorizing official

Authorization decisions are made by one or more (single or joint authorization) authorizing officials based on the authorization package. There are four types of authorization decisions:

- Authorization to operate
- Common control authorization
- Authorization to use
- Denial of authorization

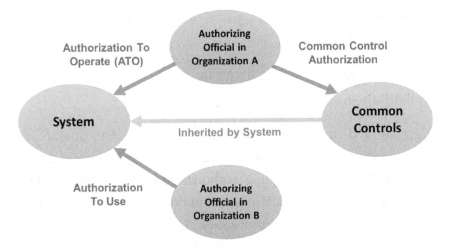

FIGURE 5-12 TYPES OF AUTHORIZATION DECISIONS

The decision of "authorization to use" is referred to as "leveraged authorization" in the superseded NIST SP 800-37 R1. Leveraged authorization is employed when a federal agency (leveraging organization) chooses to accept some or all of the information in an existing authorization package generated by another federal agency (owning organization) based on a need to use the same information resources.

Ongoing Authorization

Ongoing authorization is a risk-based decision process of determining whether or not to accept the risk of continual system authorization to operate. It typically leverages the security and privacy information generated by the continuous monitoring program.

When an information system is under the ongoing authorization, the system may be authorized on a time-driven or event-driven basis, and the authorization package is presented to the authorizing official via automated reports to provide information in the most efficient and timely manner possible.

An appropriately designed information security continuous monitoring (ISCP) strategy and program, introduced in NIST SP 800-137, supports the ongoing authorization of type, single, joint, and leveraged authorizations.

5.4   RISK GLOSSARY

5.4.1   CASCADING RISK

- The risk that materializes because of another risk or the situation where one failure leading to a chain reaction of failure.
- Cascading risks can be aggregated if there are cause and effect relationships among them.

5.4.2   INHERENT RISK

- The risk **level** or **exposure** without taking into account the actions that management has taken or might take. (ISACA, 2019)
- The expected **exposure** of the newly identified risk to which no countermeasure is applied, also known as **untreated risk** or **raw risk**.

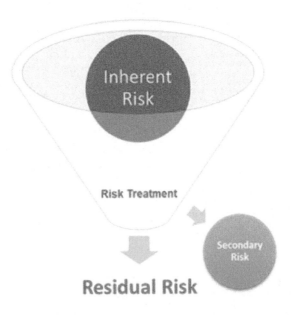

FIGURE 5-13 INHERENT RISK AND RESIDUAL RISK

5.4.3 RESIDUAL RISK

- Risk remaining **after risk treatment**, also known as **"retained risk."** (ISO Guide 73:2009)
- The risk that remains **after risk responses** have been implemented. (PMI, 2019)

5.4.4 RISK

- Risk is "the effect of uncertainty on objectives."
- Uncertainty may refer to either **likelihood** or **probability**. The likelihood is the chance of something happening in a general way, while probability is a mathematical or statistical term.
- The effect, impact, and consequence are often used interchangeably.

5.4.5 RISK AGGREGATION

- A technique to roll up several **discrete** or **lower-level** risks into a more **general** or **higher-level** risk and assess the **overall risk** of the aggregated set of discrete risks.
- Conducted primarily at Tiers 1 and 2 and occasionally at Tier 3 in terms of multi-tiered organization-wide risk management introduced in NIST SP 800-39.

5.4.6 RISK APPETITE

- Amount and type of risk that an organization is willing to pursue or retain. (ISO, 2009)
- The degree of uncertainty an organization or individual is willing to accept in anticipation of a reward. (PMI, 2019)
- Risk appetite is the amount of risk, on a broad level, an organization is willing to accept in pursuit of value. Each organization pursues various objectives to add value and

should broadly understand the risk it is willing to undertake in doing so. (Rittenberg & Martens, 2012)

5.4.7   Risk Assessment

- Overall process of risk identification, risk analysis, and risk evaluation. (ISO 31000:2009)
- Overall process of establishment of structural engineering context, definition of system, identification of hazards and consequences, risk estimation, risk evaluation and evaluation of treatment options. (ISO 13824:2009)

5.4.8   Risk Attitude

- Organization's approach to assess and eventually pursue, retain, take or turn away from risk. (ISO, 2009)
- Common risk attitudes are **risk averse**, where risk is avoided; **risk seeking**, where risk is actively sought; **risk neutral**, where risk is neither actively sought nor avoided. (APM, 2019)

5.4.9   Risk Capacity

- The amount of risk that the entity is **able** to support in pursuit of its objectives.
- Risk capacity refers to the maximum amount of risk that an organization is **able** to endure, while risk appetite is the one that an organization is **willing** to tolerate.

5.4.10 Risk Category

- A group of potential causes of risk. (PMI, 2019)
- A prompt list or a hierarchical risk breakdown structure (RBS) can be used in the risk identification process.

- STRIDE (Spoofing, Tampering, Repudiation, Information disclosure, Denial of service, and Elevation of privilege) is an example of a prompt list to identify and categorize risk.

5.4.11 RISK EXPOSURE

- Potential loss presented to an individual, project, or organization by a risk; function of the likelihood that the risk will occur and the magnitude of the consequences of its occurrence. (ISO 16085:2006)
- Product of a probability and the magnitude of a consequence, that is, an expected value or expected exposure. (ISO 24765:2017)
- Risk exposure is a measure of potential loss that can be evaluated with monetary value, a score, or scale values (e.g., High, Moderate, or Low) in terms of the likelihood, consequences, and other risk factors. The purpose of risk exposure is to prioritize risks and inform decisions.

Risk = Threat x Vulnerability

This formula is overly simplified and commonly misunderstood. Each term in the formula is elaborated as follows:

- The **Risk** should refer to "risk exposure."
- The **Threat** should refer to the "impact of a threat."
- The **Vulnerability** should refer to the "likelihood of exploiting the vulnerability."

Risk exposure is a function of the **impact** of a threat and the **likelihood** of exploiting the vulnerability. Moreover, the calculation of the function doesn't have to be multiplication.

5.4.12 RISK FACTOR

- A characteristic used in a risk model as an input to determining the level of risk in a risk assessment. (NIST, 2019)
- Risk factors in the risk model describe a risk structurally. Risk can be defined and comprehended by a risk model that entails fundamental risk factors such as **uncertainty** (e.g., risk source, event, vulnerability, likelihood, possibility, or cause) and **effect** (e.g., impact, consequence, or ramification).
- Several other risk factors can be added to define further risks such as vulnerability, failure detectability, and security control reliability and effectiveness.

5.4.13 RISK LEVEL

- The risk level is the scale of risk exposure, e.g., high, medium, and low, also known as the level of risk.
- It may sometimes refer to the origin of a risk in terms of the organization hierarchy (tiers), e.g., information systems, business processes, and organization.

5.4.14 RISK MODEL

- A key component of a risk assessment methodology (in addition to the assessment approach and analysis approach) that defines key terms and assessable risk factors. (NIST, 2019)
- A **risk model** is used to define risk in terms of predefined **risk factors**.

5.4.15 RISK OWNER

- The person responsible for monitoring the risk and for selecting and implementing an appropriate risk response strategy. (PMI, 2019)

- Entity with the accountability and authority to manage a risk. (ISO 22300:2018)

5.4.16 RISK PROFILE

- Chronological record of a risk's current and historical risk state information. (ISO 24765:2017)
- Description of any set of risks. (ISO Guide 73:2009)
- A description of the overall (identified) risk to which the enterprise is exposed. (ISACA, 2019)
- A risk profile is a summary that lists estimates for all the risks associated with a strategy, program, project or activity. Risk profiles are documented and visualized using different methods but are typically based on estimates for the probability and impact of a list of identified risks. (Spacey, 2017)

5.4.17 RISK REGISTER

- A repository in which outputs of risk management processes are recorded. (PMI, 2019)
- Record of information about identified risks; compilation for all risks identified, analyzed and evaluated in the risk assessment process, including information on the risk register includes information on likelihood, consequences, treatments and risk owners. (ISO 22300)
- Also known as risk log.

5.4.18 RISK RESPONSE

- Documented action in regard to an identified risk. (ISO 21506:2018)
- It is common to use the terms risk response and risk treatment interchangeably.

5.4.19 RISK SCORE

- An easily calculated number (the score) that reflects the level of risk in the presence of some risk factors. (Wikipedia, 2019)
- A risk scoring system defines the risk levels for each risk factor and the value associated with each risk level for an organization to measure risk to prioritize and make proper decisions.

5.4.20 RISK THRESHOLD

- The level of risk exposure **above** which risks are addressed and **below** which risks may be accepted. (PMBOK Guide — Sixth Edition)
- Condition that triggers some stakeholder action. (ISO 16085:2006)
- Different risk thresholds can be defined for each risk, risk category or combination of risks, based on differing risk criteria. (ISO 24765:2017)

5.4.21 RISK TOLERANCE

- The acceptable level of **variation** that management is willing to allow for any particular risk as the enterprise pursues its objectives. (ISACA, 2019)
- Assessed and accepted threshold levels of risk exposure that when exceeded will trigger a **risk response**. (ISO/TR 21506:2018)
- Organization's or stakeholder's readiness to **bear** the risk after risk treatment in order to achieve its objectives. (ISO, 2009)
- [deprecated] The degree of uncertainty that an organization or individual is willing to withstand. (PMI, 2019)

5.4.22 RISK TREATMENT

- Process to eliminate risk or reduce it to a tolerable level. (ISO 15026-3:2015)
- Process of selection and implementation of options to modify risk. (ISO/IEC Guide 73:2002)
- Process of selection and implementation of measures to modify risk. (ISO 16085:2006)
- Means of modifying risk. (ISO 24765:2017)
- There are four risk treatment options available for risk treatment: risk modification, risk retention, risk avoidance, and risk sharing introduced in ISO 27005.
- The term "risk treatment" is sometimes used for the measures themselves. Risk treatment measures can include avoiding, optimizing, transferring or retaining risk. (ISO/IEC 16085:2006)

5.4.23 SECONDARY RISK

- A risk that arises as a direct result of implementing a risk response. (PMI, 2019)
- Risk response is also known as risk treatment in ISO 31000 and ISO 27005.

REVIEW QUESTIONS

1. **Which of the following best applies to an information security risk?**
   A. ISO 31000
   B. COSO ERM
   C. ISO 27005
   D. PMI RMP

2. **Which of the following activities should be conducted first?**
   A. Context establishment
   B. Risk assessment
   C. Risk treatment
   D. Risk acceptance

3. **Which of the following activities relates uncertainties to objectives?**
   A. Risk analysis
   B. Risk evaluation
   C. Risk identification
   D. Risk treatment

4. **Which of the following relies on subjective judgment, experience, and intuition the most?**
   A. Quantitative analysis
   B. Qualitative analysis
   C. Semi-quantitative analysis
   D. Regression analysis

5. **Which of the following is not quantitative analysis?**
   A. Time series analysis
   B. Simulation
   C. Delphi method
   D. Monte Carlo method

6. **Which of the following refers to the repository of risk?**
   A. Risk owner
   B. Risk profile
   C. Risk register
   D. Risk map
7. **Which of the following is not done when analyzing risk?**
   A. Estimate likelihood
   B. Evaluate consequences
   C. Determine the risk score
   D. Accept a risk
8. **Which of the following is not a tier of the multi-tiered risk management?**
   A. Organization
   B. Missions/Business Processes
   C. Information Systems
   D. Strategy
9. **Which of the following component develops the risk management strategy?**
   A. Frame
   B. Assess
   C. Respond
   D. Monitor
10. **Which of the following refers to the risk that remains after risk treatment?**
    A. Inherent risk
    B. Secondary risk
    C. Residual risk
    D. Aggregate risk

6 BUSINESS CONTINUITY

"The future depends on what you do today."

- Mahatma Gandhi

6.1 CONTINUITY AND RESILIENCE

Continuity of business and **resilience to changes** are two distinct levels of **organization's ability**.

- **Continuity** is the capability to prevent, endure, and recover from disruptions.
- **Resilience** is the "ability to absorb and adapt in a changing environment." (ISO 22300:2018)
  The United States Department of Homeland Security (DHS) Risk Lexicon adds on, "resilience is the ability to quickly adapt and recover from any known or unknown changes to the environment."

FIGURE 6-1 CONTINUITY AND RESILIENCE

"**Continuity management** is essentially returning a business to 'business as usual', and nothing more. **Resilience**... not only enables organizations to continue with business as usual, but also to learn, progress and flourish... which will likely involve transformation." (Bhamra, 2015)

"In short, **business continuity** returns us to where we were before an incident but a **resilient organization** will evolve and grow from the incident." (Massie, 2018).

6.1.1 BUSINESS CONTINUITY

Definition

> **Business Continuity** is the **capability** of an organization to continue the delivery of **products and services** within acceptable time frames at predefined capacity during a **disruption**. *(ISO 22310:2019)*

- **Capability** is the "**ability** to achieve a desired effect under specified standards and conditions." (ISO/TS 18667:2018)
- **Product and service** are the "**output** or **outcome** provided by an organization to interested parties."

Business Continuity Organizations

The Organization of International Standard (ISO), the Disaster Recovery Institute (DRI), and the Business Continuity Institute (BCI) are three of the primary business continuity organizations that define industrial standards or publish professional practices for business continuity.

Org.	Standard/Practice
ISO	ISO 22301 (BCMS Standard)
BCI	BCM Lifecycle and Professional Practices
DRI	Professional Practices for BCM

TABLE 6-1 BUSINESS CONTINUITY RELATED ORGANIZATIONS

Business Continuity Certifications

Both BCI and DRI provide certification programs. BCI provides the Certification of the BCI (CBCI). DRI administer certifications such as Associate Business Continuity Planner (ABCP), Certified Functional Continuity Professional (CFCP), Certified Business Continuity Professional (CBCP), and Master Business Continuity Professional (MBCP).

Business Continuity Management (BCM) History

Business continuity management (BCM) can be traced back to as early as the 1970s when organizations were facing risks from hazards and disruptions and challenges of restoration and recovery, as a form of crisis management.

However, "the study of crisis management originated with large-scale industrial and environmental disasters in the 1980s." (Wikipedia, 2019)

- DRI and BCI are established in 1988 and 1994, respectively.
- NIST published the first Contingency Planning Guide for Federal Information Systems in 2002, which addresses system disruptions and introduces business continuity and organizational resilience planning. It was revised in 2010.
- BS 25999 was a Business Continuity Management (BCM) standard published by the British Standards Institution (BSI). It was withdrawn in 2012 (part 2) and 2013 (part 1) following the publication of the international standards ISO 22301:2012.
- ISO 22301 was revised in 2019, and ISO 22313, the guidance on the use of ISO 22301, was revised in 2020.

FIGURE 6-2 BUSINESS CONTINUITY MANAGEMENT HISTORY

6.1.2   ORGANIZATIONAL RESILIENCE

Definition

> ***Organizational resilience*** *is the* ***ability*** *of an organization to absorb and adapt in a* ***changing*** *environment. (ISO 22316:2017)*

Organizational resilience is "the ability of an organization to anticipate, prepare for, respond and adapt to incremental change and sudden disruptions in order to survive and prosper." (BSI, 2019)

Resiliency Program

Organizations develop and exercise **resilience** to reach **resiliency**, which is not a process, but an end-state for organizations. A **resiliency program** typically includes security activities such as:

1. Risk management
2. Business continuity management
3. Emergency management
4. Crisis management
5. Incident management
6. Disaster recovery
7. Critical infrastructure protection
8. Information Technologies
9. Information Security
10. Workplace recovery
11. Succession planning
12. Pandemic preparedness
13. Supply chain management
14. Human resource management

6.1.3   EVENT TAXONOMY

Definition

> **Event** is the "occurrence or change of a particular set of circumstances." (ISO 31000:2018)

As events are **uncertain** and cause **effects**, they are, in essence, **risks** or **opportunities** and **threats** to an organization.

Organizations adapt and respond to a variety of **events**, such as protecting people and the organization from **emergencies** or emergent situations, facilitating communications in **crises**, responding to **incidents**, sustaining business processes in case of short-term and long-term **disruptions**, and recovering information systems from and **disasters**.

This book classifies the terminologies mentioned above as the following diagram shows:

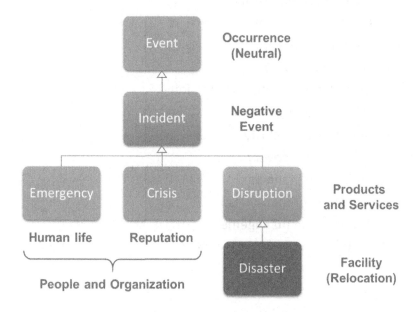

FIGURE 6-3 EVENT TAXONOMY

Incident

Event that can be, or could lead to, a **disruption**, loss, **emergency** or **crisis**. (ISO 22300:2018)

Emergency

Unintended circumstance, bearing clear and present danger to **personnel** or **property**, which requires an **immediate** response. (ISO/TR 15916:2015)

Crisis

A critical **event** that may dramatically impact an organization's profitability, **reputation**, or ability to operate if not handled appropriately or **timely**. (BRCCI, 2019)

Disruption

An **incident**, whether anticipated or unanticipated, that causes an unplanned, negative deviation from the expected delivery of **products and services** according to an organization's **objectives**. (ISO 22301:2019)

Disaster

A catastrophic incident that causes **long-term disruption** or **physical damages** at the facility level and requires the activation of recovery plans to relocate information systems **from the primary site to the alternative site**.

A sudden, unplanned catastrophic **event** causing unacceptable damage or loss. a) An event that compromises an organization's ability to provide critical functions, processes, or services for some unacceptable period of time b) An event where an organization's management invokes their recovery plans. (DRI, 2019)

6.2   ORGANIZATIONAL RESILIENCE PLANNING

6.2.1   MULTITIERED PLANNING FRAMEWORK

Organizations develop and exercise organizational resilience to protect people, interests of key stakeholders, reputation, and brand, continue essential functions and critical processes, and recover dependent information systems and resources in order to deliver products and services during any type of incident.

To develop organizational resilience, it requires comprehensive planning. NIST SP 800-39 for managing information security risk provides a multitiered framework ideal for organizational resilience planning. **Emergency planning** (added by this book) deals with the situation that needs immediate or timely and appropriate response; **continuity planning** addresses the continuous delivery of products and services, while **contingency planning** takes care of technical issues.

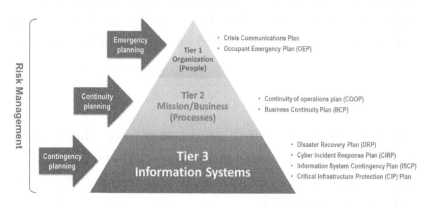

FIGURE 6-4 MULTITIERED PLANNING FRAMEWORK

The diagram above depicts the PPT strategy (people, process, and technology). As people are the organization's most valuable asset, this book places "People" at the top of the hierarchy to highlight emergencies to human life and organizational reputation.

Organizational Resilience Planning Landscape

Even though the **NIST SP 800-34 R1** guideline addresses risk at the level of information systems, it also gives an excellent introduction to the organizational resilience planning. It not only applies to the US government but also provides a reference planning framework for the private sector.

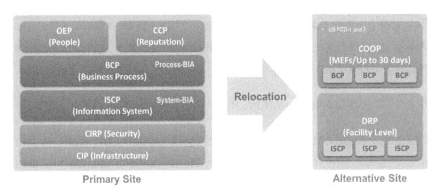

FIGURE 6-5 ORGANIZATIONAL RESILIENCE PLANNING LANDSCAPE

Summary of Plans

Plan	Key Points
BCP	Addressing mission/business processes
COOP	Addressing MEFs at an alternate site for up to 30 days; mandated by federal directives
ISCP	Addressing single information system recovery at the current or, if appropriate, an alternate location
DRP	Relocating information systems to an alternate location
CIRP	Mitigating and correcting a cyber attack
CCP	Addressing communications with personnel and the public
OEP	Minimizing injury or loss of life and protecting the property from damage
CIP	Protecting national critical infrastructure components

TABLE 6-2 SUMMARY OF PLANS

6.2.2 OCCUPANT EMERGENCY PLAN (OEP)

The OEP outlines first-response, evacuation, and shelter-in-place procedures and addresses incidents or threats to the health and safety of personnel, the environment, or property at the facility level, such as fire, bomb threat, chemical release, domestic violence in the workplace, or a medical emergency.

Evacuation procedures may require occupants of a facility to stop working and leave the building, while shelter-in-place procedures require personnel to stay inside the building rather than evacuate.

6.2.3 CRISIS COMMUNICATIONS PLAN

Crisis communication is part of **crisis management**, that "is the process by which an organization deals with a disruptive and unexpected event that threatens to harm the organization or its stakeholders. The study of crisis management originated with large-scale industrial and environmental disasters in the 1980s. It is considered to be the most important process in **public relations**." (Wikipedia, 2019)

The crisis communications plan typically designates spokespersons as the only authority for answering questions from or providing information to the public regarding emergency response.

It also establishes procedures for communications and status reports and templates for public press releases in the event of a disruption. Those procedures should be communicated to the organization's COOP and BCP planners.

6.2.4 Business Continuity Plan (BCP)

In the sector of the US **government**, BCP provides procedures for sustaining non-mission essential functions (non-MEFs) and recovering from a significant disruption **at the primary site**.

Other functions or those at a field office level may also be addressed by a BCP, which can be activated in coordination with a COOP plan if relocation to the alternate site is required.

Nongovernment organizations typically use BCPs rather than COOP plans to address disruptions of business processes and relocation. The BCP focuses on preventing and sustaining an organization's business processes during and after a disruption.

Business Continuity Policy

A **business continuity policy** initiates and charters the **business continuity program** and directs the business continuity activities so that the senior management shall be committed to the business continuity program.

The Scope of Business Continuity

There is a misconception that the scope of business continuity should account for a disaster that occurs at any location where your organization conducts its business. It is especially true when it comes to the private sector.

The scope of business continuity in practice can be determined to a narrower extent. It may include one or more products and services supported by business processes across one or more functions, business units, or the entire organization.

Business Impact Analysis

Business Impact Analysis (BIA) can be conducted at the process or system level, also known as **process-BIA** or **system-BIA**. The BIA in BCP is the process-BIA, while the BIA in ISCP is the system BIA.

The purpose of BIA is to identify **critical business processes** and **underlying or dependent resources** and evaluate the business impact of resource loss so as to prioritize the orders of resource recovery. Information systems, suppliers, manpower, and electricity are common resources. The criticality of the business process is usually expressed with **Maximum Tolerable Downtime (MTD)**, which dominates the **Recovery Time Objectives (RTOs)** of dependent resources.

Risk Assessment

Risk assessment (against the identified processes and dependent resources) typically starts after the completion of the BIA. However, risk assessment can be conducted first, then goes the BIA as long as the risk is assessed. The risk assessment shall be performed so that risks to the processes and dependent resources are identified and prioritized, the business impact of an outage of critical activities is analyzed, and appropriate actions are implemented to mitigate the risk.

Risk Treatment

After the business impact analysis and risk assessment, business continuity strategies, solutions, plans, and procedures are developed as part of risk treatment. Incident response and disaster recovery can be viewed as business continuity solutions activated by business continuity plans.

6.2.5   Continuity of Operations (COOP) Plan

Federal Directives

COOP applies to the US government departments or agencies to meet the following directives:

1. HSPD-20/NSPD-51, *National Continuity Policy*
2. FCD-1, *Federal Executive Branch National Continuity Program and Requirements*

Mission Essential Functions

A **mission** typically is something unique the organization does. On the other hand, a supporting activity is something most organizations do, such as providing IT support.

Essential functions refer to those functions an organization **MUST** continue in a continuity situation.

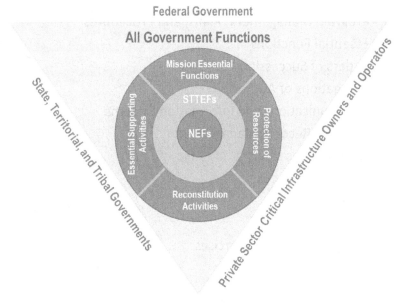

FIGURE 6-6 US GOVERNMENT FUNCTIONS

Relocation for Restoration of MEFs

COOP focuses on restoring an organization's **mission essential functions (MEF)** at an **alternate site** (at least 5 miles away from the primary site in the same region) and performing those functions for **up to 30 days** before returning to normal operations.

COOP as a specific type of plan differs from **ISCP**, **DRP**, and **BCP**. Minor threats or disruptions that do not require relocation to an alternate site are typically not addressed in a COOP plan.

Basic COOP planning process:

- Identify MEFs
- Conduct business process analysis (BPA)
- Conduct business impact analysis (BIA)
- Mitigate risks

The following are requirements that must be addressed per FCD-1:

A. Program Management, Plans, and Procedures
B. Essential Functions
C. Orders of Succession
D. Delegations of Authority
E. Communications and Information Systems
F. Essential Records Management
G. Alternate Locations
H. Human Resources
I. Devolution
J. Reconstitution
K. Test, Training, and Exercises

6.2.6   INFORMATION SYSTEM CONTINGENCY PLAN (ISCP)

As Information systems are central to CISSP (Certified <u>Information Systems</u> Security Professional), ISCP is worth more of our attention.

An ISCP is a **system-specific** plan, which provides established system recovery procedures regardless of site or location through interim measures, such as relocation to an **alternate site**, recovery using **alternate equipment**, and performance using **manual methods**.

Contingency Plan Structure

The following diagram from NIST SP 800-34 R1 depicts the structure of the ISCP.

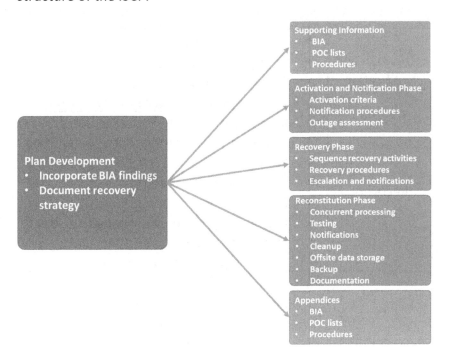

FIGURE 6-7 CONTINGENCY PLAN STRUCTURE

The seven steps in the ISCP planning process are:

1. Develop the **contingency** (not continuity) planning policy
2. Conduct the **system-level** business impact analysis (BIA)
3. Identify **preventive** controls
4. Create contingency **strategies**
5. Develop and **document** the system contingency plan
6. Ensure plan **testing, training, and exercises (TTE)**
7. Ensure plan **maintenance**

ISCP Phases

This ISCP recovers the system using a three-phase approach. The following table is a summary of major activities in each phase:

Phase	Major Activities
Activation and Notification	• Notify recovery personnel. • Conduct an outage assessment. • Activate the ISCP. • Get prepared for recovery measures.
Recovery	• Implement recovery strategies to recover high-priority system resources identified in the BIA. • Restore system capabilities. • Repair damage. • Resume operational capabilities using manual processing or an alternate system at the original or alternate site.
Reconstitution	• Confirm recovery has completed, or prepare a new location to support system processing requirements if the original facility is unrecoverable. • Validate data and functionality under the support of concurrent processing. • Deactivate the ISCP.

TABLE 6-3 ISCP PHASES

Business Impact Analysis

The goal of the ISCP is to recover the information system within the **recovery time objective (RTO)** that is constrained by the **maximum tolerable downtime (MTD)** identified by conducting the business impact analysis (BIA) at the information system level (system-BIA). The system-BIA incorporates BIA findings from the process-BIA of the BCP.

BIA is an analysis of an information system's requirements, functions, and interdependencies used to characterize system contingency requirements and priorities in the event of significant disruption.

Three steps are typically involved in accomplishing the BIA:

1. Determine business processes and recovery criticality.
2. Identify resource requirements.
3. Identify recovery priorities for system resources.

The following diagram excerpted from NSIT SP 800-34 R1 conclusively demonstrates the BIA process.

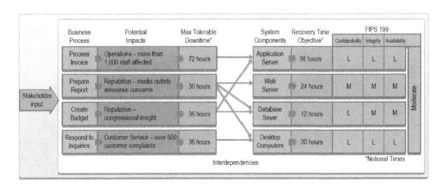

FIGURE 6-8 ANALYSIS OF BUSINESS IMPACT

Common Terminologies Used in BIA

The first version of NIST SP 800-34 used the term **Maximum Allowable Outage (MAO)** to describe the downtime threshold of the information system. To further delineate the business process and the information system downtime, **Maximum Tolerable Downtime (MTD)** and **Recovery Time Objective (RTO)** terms are used.

Downtime here typically refers to the disruption of the business process, while **outage** emphasizes the unavailability of the information system. However, terms such as **downtime**, **interruption**, and **disruption** can be used interchangeably, so do **allowable**, **acceptable**, and **tolerable**.

As various methodologies or approaches may define those terminologies differently and lead to miscommunication, the following diagram demonstrates a scenario to introduce common languages used in the analysis of business impact.

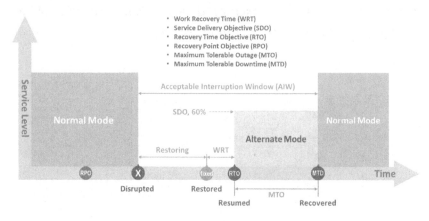

FIGURE 6-9 COMMON TERMINOLOGIES USED IN BIA

Acceptable Interruption Window (AIW)

Acceptable Interruption Window (AIW) is "the maximum period of time that a **system** can be unavailable before compromising the achievement of the enterprise's business objectives." (ISACA, 2019)

AIW is also known as the Maximum Tolerable Downtime (MTD) or Maximum Tolerable Period of Disruption (MTPD). However, the definition by ISACA emphasizes "system," while MTD or MTPD is a business term that focuses on the disruption of business processes or prioritized activities.

Work Recovery Time (WRT)

Work Recovery Time (WRT) is the "length of time needed to recover lost data, work backlog, and manually captured work once a system is recovered and repaired." (BRCCI, 2019)

WRT is typically related to the Recovery Point Objective (RPO). The shorter is the RPO; the quicker is the WRT. The sum of the repairing time and WRT should be less than the Recovery Time Objective (RTO).

Recovery Time Objective (RTO)

Recovery Time Objective (RTO) is "the amount of time allowed for the recovery of a business function or resource after a disaster occurs." (ISACA, 2019)

The recovery of a business function or resource means it meets both the ROP and Service Delivery Objective (SDO), and subject to Maximum Tolerable Outages (MTO); it is restored with the latest data and operates at an adequate level of services within the constraint of MTO.

Recovery Point Objective (RPO)

Recovery Point Objective (RPO) is "determined based on the acceptable data loss in case of a disruption of operations. It indicates the earliest point in time that is acceptable to recover the data. The RPO effectively quantifies the permissible amount of data loss in case of interruption." (ISACA, 2019)

The RPO drives the design of recovery or alternate site and backup strategy. It also affects Work Recovery Time (WRT).

Service Delivery Objective (SDO)

Service Delivery Objective (SDO) is "directly related to the business needs, it is the level of services to be reached during the alternate mode until the normal situation is restored." (ISACA, 2019)

When a system is resumed within the RTO and RPO, it operates in alternate mode, in which the system should provide an adequate level of services and meet the SDO.

Maximum Tolerable Outage (MTO)

Maximum Tolerable Outage (MTO) is the maximum time that an enterprise can support processing in alternate mode. (ISACA, 2019)

The alternate mode is not viable for long-term operations. MTO sets the objective of the time period for the business continuity solutions to transit to normal mode.

Maximum Tolerable Downtime (MTD)

See Acceptable Interruption Window (AIW).

6.2.7   DISASTER RECOVERY PLAN (DRP)

According to NIST SP 800-34 R1, the DRP is primarily a site-specific plan developed with procedures to move operations of one or more information systems from a damaged or uninhabitable location to a temporary alternate location.

The DRP is a **site-specific** plan that only addresses disruptions requiring **relocation**. It primarily applies to major or physical disruptions that deny access to the primary facility infrastructure for an extended period. It recovers one or more information systems per the Recovery Time Objective (RTO), Recovery Point Objective (RPO), and Service Delivery Objective (SDO) at a temporary alternate location.

The DRP may comprise multiple information system contingency plans (ISCPs) that recover impacted individual systems once the alternate facility has been established. The ISCP differs from a DRP primarily in that its procedures are developed for recovery of the system regardless of location; it can be activated at the system's current or alternate location.

A BCP or COOP plan may be supported by the DRP to recover supporting systems for mission/business processes or mission essential functions at an alternate location.

6.2.8   CYBER INCIDENT RESPONSE PLAN

The capability of responding to incidents is a core component of business continuity. The cyber incident response plan establishes procedures to address cyberattacks against an organization's information systems that support mission/business processes. This plan may be included as an appendix of the BCP.

There are various incident response methodologies or approaches. NIST SP 800-61 Rev. 2, Computer Security Incident Handling Guide, provides guidance on establishing a cyber incident response capability and plan. It introduces an incident response life cycle as follows:

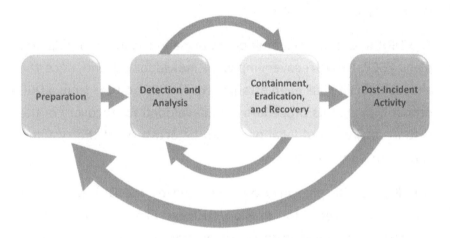

FIGURE 6-10 INCIDENT RESPONSE LIFE CYCLE

Preparation work is often overlooked, but it emphasizes not only establishing an incident response capability but also preventing incidents. Tools and resources for incident handlers should be prepared, such as communications, facilities, incident analysis hardware and software, and so forth. Besides, prevention is better than treatment. Keeping the number of incidents reasonably low is crucial to the business continuity of the organization.

Incident Handling Checklist

The following table of Incident Handling Checklist is excerpted from NIST SP 800-61 R2.

#	Action	Check
	Detection and Analysis	
1.	Determine whether an incident has occurred	
1.1	Analyze the precursors and indicators	
1.2	Analyze the precursors and indicators	
1.3	Perform research (e.g., search engines, knowledge base)	
1.4	As soon as the handler believes an incident has occurred, begin documenting the investigation and gathering evidence	
2.	Prioritize handling the incident based on the relevant factors (functional impact, information impact, recoverability effort, etc.)	
3.	Report the incident to the appropriate internal personnel and external organizations	
	Containment, Eradication, and Recovery	
4.	Acquire, preserve, secure, and document evidence	
5.	Contain the incident	
6.	Eradicate the incident	
6.1	Identify and mitigate all vulnerabilities that were exploited	
6.2	Remove malware, inappropriate materials, and other components	
6.3	If more affected hosts are discovered (e.g., new malware infections), repeat the Detection and Analysis steps (1.1, 1.2) to identify all other affected hosts, then contain (5) and eradicate (6) the incident for them	
7.	Recover from the incident	
7.1	Return affected systems to an operationally ready state	
7.2	Confirm that the affected systems are functioning normally	
7.3	If necessary, implement additional monitoring to look for future related activity	
	Post-Incident Activity	
8.	Create a follow-up report	
9.	Hold a lessons-learned meeting (mandatory for major incidents, optional otherwise)	

TABLE 6-4 INCIDENT HANDLING CHECKLIST

Incident Management in the CISSP Exam Outline

The following image is a snapshot from the CISSP Exam Outline about incident management. It is worthy of note that outline bullets imply but do not impose a strict logical sequence or process. Those topics, if read in series, seemingly conflict with the NIST incident response life cycle in some aspects.

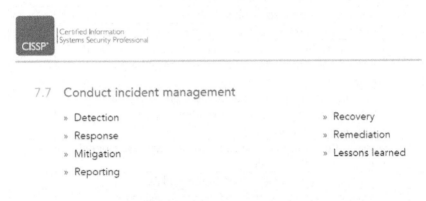

7.7   Conduct incident management

» Detection   » Recovery
» Response   » Remediation
» Mitigation   » Lessons learned
» Reporting

FIGURE 6-11 INCIDENT MANAGEMENT IN THE CISSP EXAM OUTLINE

A Modified Incident Management Model

As various incident management approaches may clash, this book summarizes and introduces a modified model based on the NIST incident response life cycle as the following diagram shows:

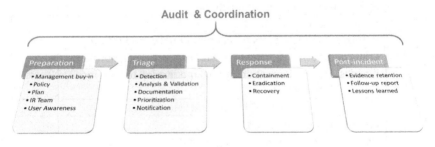

FIGURE 6-12 A MODIFIED INCIDENT MANAGEMENT MODEL

6.2.9   CRITICAL INFRASTRUCTURE PROTECTION (CIP) PLAN

The Critical Infrastructure Protection (CIP) plan is specific to the protection of the national infrastructure, or CIKR, of the United States.

According to NIST SP 800-34 R1, critical infrastructure and key resources (CIKR) are those components of the national infrastructure that are deemed so vital that their loss would have a debilitating effect of the safety, security, economy, and/or health of the United States. A CIP plan is a set of policies and procedures that serve to protect and recover these national assets and mitigate risks and vulnerabilities.

This plan may not be applicable to most of the private sector.

6.3   BUSINESS CONTINUITY MANAGEMENT

Definition

> ***Business Continuity Management*** *is a "holistic management process* **that** *identifies potential threats to an organization and the impacts to business operations those threats, if realized, might cause, and* **which** *provides a framework for building organizational resilience with the capability of an effective response that safeguards the interests of its key stakeholders, reputation, brand and value-creating activities." (ISO 22300:2018)*

In essence, business continuity management provides a framework for building organizational resilience, even though it uses "business continuity" literally.

However, ISO 22313:2020 simplifies the definition as a "process of implementing and maintaining business continuity in order to prevent loss and prepare for, mitigate and manage disruptions."

A process is a "set of interrelated or interacting activities which transforms inputs into outputs."

6.3.1 ISO 22301 BCMS Standard

Definition

---

*A **business continuity management system (BCMS)** is a management system that "**develops business continuity** appropriate to the amount and type of impact that the organization may or may not accept following a disruption." (ISO 22301:2019)*

A **management system** is a set of interrelated or interacting **elements** of an organization to establish policies and objectives, and **processes** to achieve those objectives. (ISO 22301:2019)

The **management system elements** establish the organization's structure, roles and responsibilities, planning, operation, policies, practices, rules, beliefs, objectives and processes to achieve those objectives. (ISO 22300:2018)

The scope of a management system can include:

- The whole of the organization
- Specific and identified functions of the organization
- Specific and identified sections of the organization
- One or more functions across a group of organizations

ISO 22301:2019

ISO 22301:2019, Security and resilience – Business continuity management systems – Requirements, is a management system standard for business continuity published by the International Organization for Standardization (ISO).

BCMS Components

A BCMS includes the following components:

- Business continuity policy
- Competent people with defined responsibilities
- Management processes
- Documented information supporting operational control and enabling performance evaluation
- Other relevant BCM processes

Management Processes

1. Policy
2. Planning
3. Implementation and operation
4. Performance assessment
5. Management review
6. Continual improvement

Other Relevant BCM Processes

1. Incident response
2. Emergency management
3. Crisis management
4. Disaster recovery
5. Workplace recovery
6. Succession planning
7. Pandemic preparedness
8. Supply chain management

6.3.2   BCI BCM LIFECYCLE

The Business Continuity Institute (BCI) proposed the BCM Lifecycle that comprises six stages, each of which implements a Professional Practice. It also releases the **Good Practice Guideline (GPG)** to address the six Professional Practices.

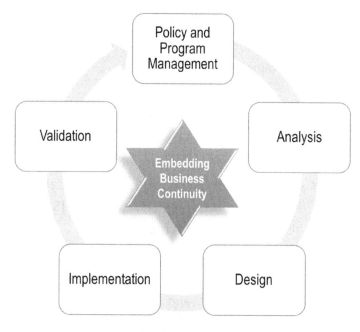

FIGURE 6-13 BCI BCM LIFECYCLE

Embedding Business Continuity

The Embedding stage defines how to integrate business continuity practice into business as usual activities and organizational culture using a collaborative approach to improve organizational resilience.

This stage employs an organization-wide approach and places emphasis on understanding organizational culture, adapting to change, and engaging with individuals and groups more effectively.

Policy and Program Management

The Policy and Program Management stage establishes the organization's business continuity policy and the implementation approach through an ongoing cycle of activities within the business continuity program.

This stage also emphasizes the importance of relating the business continuity policy to other relevant policies and how it supports the organization's strategic objectives.

Analysis

The Analysis stage reviews and assesses an organization to identify its objectives, how it functions, and the constraints of its operating environment. The primary technique used to analyze the organization is the Business Impact Analysis (BIA). A risk assessment is also undertaken at this stage.

Design

The Design stage identifies and selects business continuity solutions. The design process evolves from the strategic, tactical to operation level leads to a more organization-wide.

The Design stage provides examples of the types of resources required for a range of well-established business continuity solutions that can be used within an organization.

This stage includes further considerations such as remote working and a sub-section on the consolidation of the continuity solutions designed for improved efficiency.

Implementation

The Implementation stage implements the solutions agreed in the Design stage. Business continuity plans, as part of the solutions, include details of the priorities, procedures, responsibilities, and resources required to manage an incident and return the organization to pre-agreed acceptable levels within the planned time frames.

Validation

The goal of the Validation stage is to improve the BC program continuously and enhance the organizational resilience by confirming if the program meets the objectives of the BC policy and the plans in place are effective. Exercises, maintenance, and review are vital activities to validate the business continuity program.

6.3.3   DRI PROFESSIONAL PRACTICES

The Professional Practices for Business Continuity Management is a body of knowledge (BOK) designed to assist in the development, implementation, and maintenance of business continuity programs. It is created and maintained by Disaster Recovery Institute International and intended to serve as a tool for conducting assessments of existing programs.

There are ten **Professional Practices**:

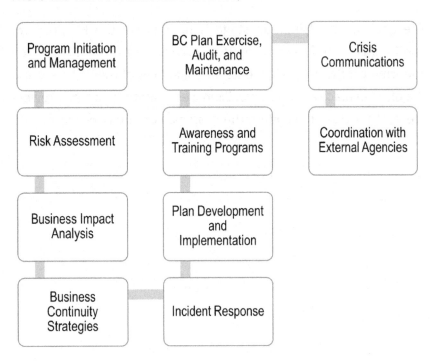

FIGURE 6-14 DRI PROFESSIONAL PRACTICES

6.4   BUSINESS CONTINUITY PROGRAM

Definition

> ***Business continuity program*** *is the "ongoing management and governance process supported by top management and appropriately resourced* **to implement and maintain business continuity management.***" (ISO 22300:2018)*

The primary purpose of the **business continuity program** is to implement and maintain **business continuity management (BCM)**, which provides a framework for building **organizational resilience.** If the BCM within the defined scope is compliant with the ISO 22301 standard, it is also knowns as a **business continuity management system (BCMS)**.

The business continuity program is an instrument of strategy execution. As developing organizational resilience has been an essential strategic issue, it is often addressed in a strategy that is accompanied by the **business continuity policy** to initiate and direct the **business continuity program.**

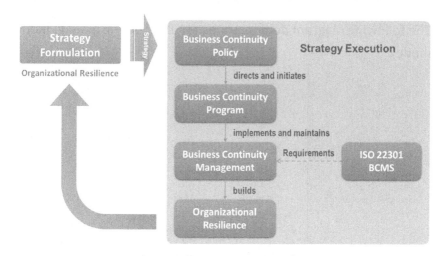

FIGURE 6-15 BUSINESS CONTINUITY OVERVIEW

ISO Generic Management Model

Developing business continuity starts with analyzing the **organization**, and its **context** to determine internal and external issues and **interested parties (stakeholders)** to identifies their needs, expectations, and requirements. **Intended outcomes** and **scope** are then derived based on the analysis result.

Top management issues the **business continuity policy**, so that the **business continuity program** is initiated, projects within the program are authorized, and the team is established. All levels of management should demonstrate **leadership** and **commitment** across the lifecycle of the business continuity program.

The **business continuity objectives** are established in line with the organization's overall objectives, business continuity policy, Intended outcomes, and scope. A **program management plan** is developed to direct program activities. Resources allocation, performance measurement, management reviews, corrective actions, and continual improvement are conducted to produce optimal intended outcomes.

The following diagram demonstrates the ISO generic management model.

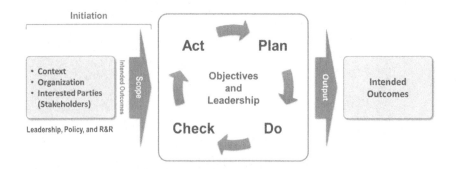

FIGURE 6-16 ISO GENERIC MANAGEMENT MODEL

The book focuses on the ISO Generic Management Model. However, there are some differences between the ISO model and the business continuity planning approach introduced in the Sybex Official (ISC)² CISSP Study Guide (OSG) as the following table shows.

The main difference is that, risk identification is part of the business impact assessment (BIA) in the OSG approach, but risk assessment can be conducted before or after BIA in the ISO model.

Stages	Activities
Project Scope and Planning	• Business Organization Analysis • BCP Team Selection • Resource Requirements • Legal and Regulatory Requirements
Business Impact Assessment	• Identify Priorities • Risk Identification • Likelihood Assessment • Impact Assessment • Resource Prioritization
Continuity Planning	• Strategy development • Provisions and processes
Plan Approval and Implementation	• Plan approval • Plan implementation • Training and education • BCP Documentation
Plan Validation	• Testing and Exercises

TABLE 6-5 THE OFFICIAL (ISC)² STUDY GUIDE BCP APPROACH

6.4.1   INITIATION

Developing business continuity begins with understanding the internal and external context of the organization and the requirements of interested parties. The results determine the **scope** defined in terms of **products and services** and **parts of the organization**.

Issues and requirements that shape the intended outcomes and scope may come from, but not limited to, the following factors:

- Internal context
  - o Organizational purpose and requirements
  - o Products and services provided
  - o Processes employed
  - o Size and structure of the organization
- External context
  - o legal and regulatory requirements
  - o Industrial requirements
- Interested parties
  - o Needs, expectations, and requirements

There are a variety of interested parties, such as suppliers, citizens, customers, distributors, shareholders, investors, owners, insurers, government, regulators, service providers, competitors, media, commentators, trade groups, neighbors, pressure groups, emergency services, other response agencies, transport services, and workforce dependents.

Intended Outcomes

Examples of intended outcomes may include:

- Continuity of key products and services are ensured
- An effective incident management capability is established
- Employees are trained to respond effectively to incidents and receive adequate support and communications
- Requirements of interested parties are understood and able to be delivered
- The supply chain is secured
- The organization's reputation is protected
- The organization is compliant with legal and regulatory requirements

Scoping

Scoping is the process of scope definition driven by the intended outcomes. It starts with identifying **products and services** and **organization units** as the following sample company, Amicliens, depicts. The scope may include all or some of the elements.

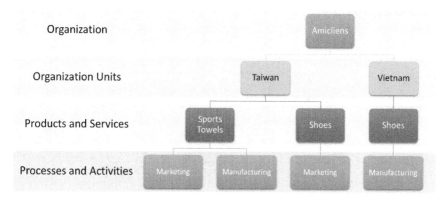

FIGURE 6-17 BUSINESS CONTINUITY SCOPING

Business Continuity Policy

The business continuity policy is the evidence that top management demonstrates its leadership and commitment to satisfying applicable requirements and continual improvement; it should be documented, communicated within the organization, and available to interested parties. Top management should ensure that the business continuity policy is appropriate to the purpose of the organization, provides a framework for setting business continuity objectives, and identifies relevant roles and assign responsibilities and delegate authorities to them.

Program Initiation

The **business continuity policy** can serve as the **program policy** to initiate and charter the business continuity program. After the business continuity policy is issued, the business continuity program is initiated; projects within the program are authorized; the business continuity team is established with specific roles, responsibilities, and authorities. The following diagram introduces the concept of program strategy alignment: (Project Management Institute, 2017)

FIGURE 6-18 PROGRAM STRATEGY ALIGNMENT

6.4.2 PLAN

The "Plan" stage is about exercising leadership to establish business continuity policy, objectives, controls, processes, and procedures relevant to improving business continuity, and provisioning resources for operations to deliver results that align with the organization's overall objectives.

Even though analyzing the context of the organization and interested parties and setting out the business continuity policy are commonly treated as part of the "Plan" stage, this book separates it into the "Initiation" stage to cope with the concept of program management.

Leadership

Leadership is about how the role of management demonstrates commitment, defining policy and establishing roles, responsibilities, and authorities. Management commitment may be demonstrated by operational involvement through steering committees, the inclusion of business continuity as a standing item at management meetings, and so forth.

Support activities typically include elements like resources, competence, awareness, communication, and documented information. Resources refer to "all assets (including plant and equipment), people, skills, technology, premises, and supplies and information (whether electronic or not) that an organization has to have available to use, when needed, in order to operate and meet its objective." (ISO 22301:2019)

Program Risk Management

Managing the risk of the business continuity program itself (not the operational risk of business continuity) and establishing the business continuity objectives determine the effectiveness of the program.

The analysis result of the "Initiation" stage can serve as the input of determining risk to the program itself (not the risk of business continuity). The risk may bring a negative or positive effect (threats or opportunities) on the program. Opportunities should also be considered. Risks can arise from:

- Lack of leadership and commitment from top management
- Insufficient funding
- Poorly documented information
- Lack of people with demonstrated competence
- The inadequate management review process
- Inability to meet business continuity requirements of new markets

The organization should plan the actions needed to address these risks and implement them at the "Do" stage.

Business Continuity Objectives

Business continuity objectives are derived and defined based on the framework laid in the business continuity policy. ISO 22313 gives some examples of business continuity objectives as follows:

- Top management will allocate the necessary resources to ensure that business continuity management is established by [date] for all products and services.
- The COO will engage with consultants to achieve certification against ISO 22301 by [date] for named products and services.

- The CIO will work with our vendors to shorten the recovery time of activities supporting named products and services by 10 %. This will be achieved by [date].

Program Planning

Planning for the business continuity program is a crucial step that follows the initiation of the program. A program management plan (the "management plan") to achieve the business continuity objectives is developed. This plan is the key output created during program planning and may be combined into one plan or multiple plans that include the following subsidiary documents: (Project Management Institute, 2017)

- Benefits management plan
- Stakeholder engagement plan
- Governance plan
- Change management plan
- Communications management plan
- Financial management plan
- Information management plan
- Procurement management plan
- Quality management plan
- Resource management plan
- Risk management plan
- Schedule management plan
- Scope management plan
- Program roadmap

6.4.3   Do

The "Do" stage identifies, implements, and operates the **processes** for establishing and maintaining **business continuity**, which addresses the continual delivery of an organization's most critical products and services. A process is a set of activities. An activity can be a task or a set of tasks. The term "business" can broadly refer to those **activities** supporting the delivery of **products and services** vital to the **purposes** of the organization's existence.

Purpose of the Organization

An organization achieves its purpose by delivering its **products and services** to customers, which relies on **prioritized activities** (also known as critical, essential, vital, or key activities), **supporting activities and dependencies**, and other **assets and resources**. **Dependencies** of prioritized activities may include people, information and data, buildings, workplaces and associated utilities, equipment and consumables, ICT systems, transportation and logistics, finance, and partners and the supply chain.

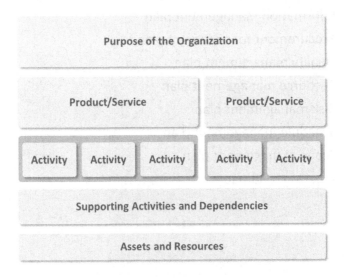

FIGURE 6-19 PURPOSE OF THE ORGANIZATION

Business Continuity Management

Leadership and the **business continuity objectives** drive the business continuity management, which comprises processes at the operational level, as depicted in the following diagram.

FIGURE 6-20 BUSINESS CONTINUITY MANAGEMENT PROCESSES

1. Operational Planning and Control

The organization should determine, plan, implement, and control the **processes** needed to establish and maintain **business continuity management** and implement the actions that address the risk to the program.

The business continuity management processes, as the above diagram shows, are introduced in ISO 22313:2020. The organization may adopt a recognized **project management** method to ensure that business continuity management is effectively managed.

2. Business Impact Analysis and Risk Assessment

The outcomes of **business impact analysis (BIA)** and **risk assessment** enable the organization to identify **business continuity strategies and solutions**. They should be reviewed at planned intervals and when there are significant changes within the organization or the context in which it operates.

The order in which business impact analysis and risk assessment are performed is not prescribed as long as the risks to its prioritized activities are assessed.

FIGURE 6-21 BUSINESS CONTINUITY EVALUATION

Business Impact Analysis

Business impact analysis (BIA) is the process of analyzing the impact **over time** of a disruption of the delivery of products and services on the organization. The evaluation criteria for determining **prioritized activities** that support the delivery of products and services includes the **types of impact** and **time frames**. There are various types of impact or impact categories, such as financial, reputational, operational, legal and regulatory, contractual, business objectives, and so forth. Disruption can be sudden or gradual and brings about one or more types of impact.

For example, the impact over time upon the capacity of operations can be illustrated by the following two diagrams:

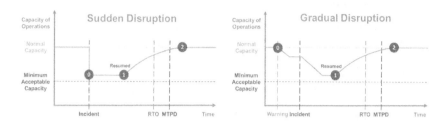

FIGURE 6-22 BUSINESS CONTINUITY WITH SUDDEN AND GRADUAL DISRUPTION

Top management should determine the thresholds that are unacceptable to the organization in terms of impact and time.

- **Maximum Tolerable Period of Disruption (MTPD)** is the time that the organization would take for impacts to become unacceptable. It is also known as Maximum Tolerable Downtime (MTD).
- **Minimum Business Continuity Objective (MBCO)** is the minimum level of product or service that is acceptable to the organization.
- **Recovery Time Objective (RTO)** is the time frame for resuming an activity.
- **Recovery Point Objective (RPO)** is the point up to which information and data used by an activity are restored to enable the activity to operate upon resumption.

The process for analyzing business impacts should include:

1. Define **evaluation criteria** for determining prioritized activities, including **types of impact** and **time frames**.
2. Identify **activities** that support the delivery of the products and services.

3. Assess the impacts over time from disruption of **these activities** using the evaluation criteria defined in Step 1.
4. Determine the MTPD.
5. Determine the RTO within MTPD for resuming activities at specified minimum acceptable capacities.
6. Identify **prioritized activities**.
7. Identify the **dependencies** of prioritized activities.
8. Identify **interdependencies** of prioritized activities.

Risk Assessment

As disruption of activities can cause the delivery of products and services to be impacted, prioritized activities need business continuity solutions in place **before** disrupted and also need urgent actions to resume **when** interrupted because failure to do so in time could result in unacceptable levels of adverse impact.

The purpose of the risk assessment is to identify, analyze, and evaluate the risks of prioritized activities and their dependencies, so that appropriate business continuity strategies and solutions can be formulated to address these risks.

ISO 31000, introduced in 3.4.4 ISO 31000, sets out the principles of risk management and associated guidelines. Risk assessment comprises three sub-processes:

- **Risk identification** is the process of identifying uncertainties that will impact the objectives.
- **Risk analysis** is the process of determining the risk score or exposure by estimating the likelihood and consequences of risk.
- **Risk evaluation** is the process of decision making based on the acceptance criteria to determine if a risk needs further actions or treatment.

3. Business Continuity Strategies and Solutions

Organizations identify and select business continuity strategies and develop solutions to mitigate risk to the prioritized activities and their dependencies with considerations of costs and benefits based on the result of business impact analysis and the risk assessment.

FIGURE 6-23 BUSINESS CONTINUITY STRATEGIES AND SOLUTIONS

Business continuity strategies are possible ways to address business continuity requirements; for example, outsourcing activities to a partner, providing remote working capabilities for employees, purchasing insurance, or building alternate sites.

A business continuity strategy may comprise one or more business continuity solutions, and a business continuity solution can be used for more than one strategy. For example, a relocation strategy may include solutions such as emergency transport, network redirection, alternate staffing, and so forth. Selected business continuity solutions in a business continuity strategy can prevent and sustain the delivery of products and services from disruption and resume operations at an **acceptable capacity** and within **agreed time frames**.

4. Business Continuity Plans and Procedures

Organizations identify and document business continuity plans and procedures based on the output of the selected strategies and solutions. Business continuity plans comprise different types of procedures. 6.2 Organizational Resilience Planning addresses a variety of plans introduced in NIST SP 800-34 R1.

A business continuity plan is a "documented information that guides an organization to **respond** to disruption and **resume**, **recover** and **restore** the delivery of products and services consistent with its business continuity objectives." It can be used, when required, to activate business continuity solutions.

A business continuity plan typically includes:

- The purpose, scope, and objectives
- Roles and responsibilities
- Actions to implement the solutions
- Activation criteria and procedures
- Implementation procedures
- Communication requirements and procedures
- Internal and external interdependencies and interactions
- Resource requirements
- Reporting requirements
- Information flow and documentation processes

Response Structure

Business continuity plans set out how teams will respond to disruptions and resume activities. The following example of teams and possible roles and responsibilities is an excerpt from ISO 22313:2020.

Team	Role	Responsibilities
• Site Emergency Response • Facilities Management • Security	• Emergency Response	• Life Safety • Damage Limitation
• Damage Assessment	• Damage Assessment	• Damage Assessment
• Incident Management	• Incident Mgmt. and Control	• Incident Mgmt.
• Crisis Management • Senior Management	• Strategic Decision-making • Communication during Incident	• Strategic Mgmt. • Crisis Management • Communications • Public Relations
• Communications	• Communication during Incident	• Communications • Public Relations
• ICT recovery	• Recovering ICT Systems and Infrastructure	• ICT Disaster Recovery
• Finance • Administrative	• General and Financial Administration	• Finance and Administration
• Human Resources • Occupational Health	• Welfare and Special needs • Interested Party Well-being	• Human Resources • Safety and Welfare
• Salvage • Facilities • ICT • Security	• Salvage of facilities, ICT Systems, and Data • Security	• Salvage and Security
• Business Continuity	• Resume disrupted activities	• Coordinate Resumption • Manage Resources

TABLE 6-6 EXAMPLES OF TEAMS AND POSSIBLE ROLES AND RESPONSIBILITIES

5. Exercise Program

The exercise program validates the effectiveness of its business continuity strategies, solutions, plans, and procedures, identifies areas for improvement, and develops teamwork, competency, confidence, and knowledge. It is not a one-time initiative but performed over time. The program should exercise to validate:

- procedures by engaging all related stakeholders,
- business continuity arrangements (e.g., command centers and work areas),
- the recovery of the ICT infrastructure, and
- response teams.

Exercises suggested in ISO 22313:2020 are summarized as follows:

Category	Exercise	Scenario	Location	Duration	Feature
Discussion	Plan review	N/A	On-site	1 h to 2 h	• Review of plans and procedures • Informal review
Simulation	Table-top	Simple	On-site	2 h to 3 h	• Review of strategies and solutions • First formal exercise
			Off-site	2 h to 3 h	• Alternative premises • Command center
	Workshop	Complex	Off-site	3 h to 5 h	One or more plans
				3 h to 5 h	One or more locations
			Full scale	-	Entire organization

FIGURE 6-24 SUMMARY OF BUSINESS CONTINUITY EXERCISES

The purpose of **discussion-based** exercises is to familiarize participants with business continuity plans and procedures in a low-stress environment, while **simulation-based** ones are more realistic and challenging.

Exercises, including **tests**, are activities designed to examine the organization's ability to respond, recover, and continue to perform assigned business functions effectively when faced with specific disruptive **scenarios**.

- A **test** is a unique and particular type of exercise, which incorporates an expectation of a pass or fail element within the goal or objectives of the exercise being planned.
- A **scenario** is a pre-planned storyline that drives an exercise, as well as the stimuli used to achieve exercise project performance objectives.

A **drill** is an activity that practices a particular skill and often involves repeating the same thing several times. For example, fire drill to practice safely evacuating a building on fire.

6. Evaluation

Business impact analysis, risk assessment, strategies and solutions, and plans and procedures should be evaluated over time based on the exercise results, post-incident reviews, and organizational dynamics through self-assessments or internal or external audits to ensure their suitability, adequacy, and effectiveness.

According to ISO 22303, evaluations should verify that:

- All products and services within the scope are covered by business continuity solutions.
- Business continuity solutions are effective and up-to-date.
- Exercise programs are effective.
- Improvements are incorporated into business continuity solutions and procedures.
- Training and awareness program is implemented.
- The business continuity arrangements that suppliers and partners have in place for dependencies of prioritized activities are appropriate and adequate.
- The organization is compliant with applicable legal and regulatory requirements.
- Change control processes operate effectively.

6.4.4   CHECK

The "Check" stage evaluates performance against business continuity policy and objectives, reports the results to management for review, and determines and authorizes actions for correction and improvement.

Performance Evaluation

Performance indicators and procedures for monitoring, measuring, analyzing, and evaluating the performance and effectiveness should be in place. Documented information of all periodic evaluations and their results should also be retained. Conducting internal audits at planned intervals is standard practice for this purpose.

An audit program should be established to direct the planning and conduct of audits with considerations of risk assessment and impact analysis, the results of past audits, and other relevant factors.

Internal audits may be performed by the internal audit department, audit committee, or external party selected by the organization. The results are submitted to top management for review and authorization for actions.

Management Review

Management review provides top management with the opportunity to evaluate over time the suitability, adequacy, and effectiveness of business continuity management.

Management review can be advisable or formal; it can be conducted at planned intervals or triggered by sector/industry trends, regulatory requirements, or incident experience.

According to ISO 22303, management review should include an appraisal of:

- the status of actions from previous reviews;
- the performance of the management system, including trends apparent from nonconformities and corrective actions, the results of monitoring and measurement, and audit findings;
- changes to the supply chain and effectiveness of supply chain continuity arrangements;
- other changes to the organization and its context and feedback from interested parties that could impact the management system;
- opportunities for continual improvement.

6.4.5 ACT

The "Act" stage maintains and improves business continuity management by taking authorized actions for correction and improvement. Corrective actions address deficiencies and ensure intended functions, while continual improvement pursues a higher level of efficiency and effectiveness.

Corrective Actions

The organization should identify deficiencies or nonconformities (instances of non-fulfillment of a requirement), contain and prevent further occurrence of the situation, investigate into root causes to avoid recurring, develop a corrective action plan, take action to correct them, and deal with their consequences. Nonconformities should be identified in a timely manner and stated in a well-defined nonconformity statement.

Continual improvement

The efficiency, effectiveness, suitability, and adequacy of business continuity management can be improved continuously across the PDCA lifecycle based on the results of the evaluation, audits, and management review.

According to ISO 22303, opportunities for continual improvement can be identified through a defined process and come from changes in:

- The internal and external context of the organization
- the means of production or delivery (e.g., technological change, infrastructure improvements);
- evolving methodologies or the availability of new recovery methods (e.g., new standby facilities or network technology);
- technology and practices, including new tools and techniques.

REVIEW QUESTIONS

1. **Which of the following best describes "continuity," except?**
   A. the capability to prevent disruptions
   B. the capability to endure disruptions
   C. the capability to recover from disruptions
   D. the capability to adapt to changes

2. **Which of the following events most relates to reputation?**
   A. Incident
   B. Emergency
   C. Crisis
   D. Disaster

3. **Which of the following relates to information systems?**
   A. Business planning
   B. Emergency planning
   C. Continuity planning
   D. Contingency planning

4. **Which of the following plans outlines first-response procedures?**
   A. Occupant Emergency Plan (OEP)
   B. Disaster Recovery Plan (DRP)
   C. Business Continuity Plan (BCP)
   D. Crisis Communications Plan

5. **Which of the following plans is least related to relocation?**
   A. Information System Contingency Plan (ISCP)
   B. Disaster Recovery Plan (DRP)
   C. Occupant Emergency Plan (OEP)
   D. Continuity of Operations (COOP) Plan

6. **Which of the following organizations is least related to business continuity?**

A. ISO

B. BCI

C. DRI

D. PMI

7. **Which of the following is the best instrument to charter a business continuity program?**

A. Risk appetite

B. Interested parties

C. Policy

D. Project manager

8. **Which of the following activities will not be conducted in the initiation stage of the business continuity program?**

A. Identify applicable laws and regulations

B. Analyze the organization

C. Collect business requirements

D. Conduct business impact analysis

9. **Which of the following activities is conducted first?**

A. Risk assessment first, then business impact analysis

B. Business impact analysis first, then the risk assessment

C. In any sequence at the discretion of management

D. In any sequence as long as the risk is assessed

10. **Which of the following elements is least likely to be included in the scope of the business continuity program?**

A. Organizational parts

B. Products

C. Services

D. Strategies

ANSWERS TO REVIEW QUESTIONS

Chapter 1

1. D. OSCP
2. D. None of the above
3. D. CSSLP
4. D. Certified Information Systems Security Professional
5. D. Discrete and unstructured knowledge points
6. A. The CISSP Certification Exam Outline
7. A. Security and Risk Management
8. D. Business strategies
9. A. One canon
10. D. Use rote memory

Chapter 2

1. B. FISMA
2. D. Appetite
3. D. State Machine
4. A. Threat
5. B. End users
6. C. Business value
7. D. Data steward
8. C. Configure a printer as "Secret"
9. D. Availability
10. A. Goals or objectives

Chapter 3

1. D. The nomination of board members
2. C. Audit committee
3. C. Exit interview
4. B. Development/Acquisition
5. C. Risk is the effect of uncertainty on objectives
6. A. Risk exposure
7. D. CMMI
8. B. Risk treatment
9. C. Risk acceptance
10. D. Audit

Chapter 4

1. B. Business strategy
2. A. Strategic alignment
3. B. Mission statement
4. D. Action plans
5. C. Project
6. C. Policy
7. C. Program
8. D. All of the above
9. D. Change requests should always be approved.
10. C. Strategic planning

Chapter 5

1. C. ISO 27005
2. A. Context establishment
3. C. Risk identification
4. B. Qualitative analysis
5. C. Delphi method
6. C. Risk register
7. D. Accept a risk
8. D. Strategy
9. A. Frame
10. C. Residual risk

Chapter 6

1. D. the capability to adapt to changes
2. C. Crisis
3. D. Contingency planning
4. A. Occupant Emergency Plan (OEP)
5. C. Occupant Emergency Plan (OEP)
6. D. PMI
7. C. Policy
8. D. Conduct business impact analysis
9. D. In any sequence as long as the risk is assessed
10. D. Strategies

REFERENCES

APM. (2019). *Risk context*. Retrieved from Association for Project Management: https://www.apm.org.uk/body-of-knowledge/delivery/risk-management/risk-context/

Bhamra, R. (2015). *Organisational Resilience: Concepts, Integration, and Practice*. CRC Press.

BRCCI. (2019). *Glossary*. Retrieved from BRCCI: https://www.brcci.org/index.php/business-continuity-and-disaster-recovery-glossary

BSI. (2019). *What is Organizational Resilience?* Retrieved from The British Standards Institution: https://www.bsigroup.com/en-GB/our-services/Organizational-Resilience/

Chapple, M., Stewart, J. M., & Gibson, D. (2018). *(ISC)2 CISSP Certified Information Systems Security Professional Official Study Guide 8th Edition*. Sybex.

Chen, K. D., & Wu, A. (2016). *The Structure of Board Committees*.

DRI. (2019). *The DRI International Glossary for Resilience*. Retrieved from DRI International, Inc.: https://drii.org/resources/viewglossary

ENISA. (2015, February 9). *Threat Landscape for Smart Home and Media Convergence*. Retrieved from European Union Agency for Network and Information Security (ENISA): https://www.enisa.europa.eu/publications/threat-landscape-for-smart-home-and-media-convergence

Gartner. (2013, May 16). *Definition: Threat Intelligence.* Retrieved from Gartner: https://www.gartner.com/en/documents/2487216/definit ion-threat-intelligence

Gartner. (2020). *User Provisioning.* Retrieved from Gartner Glossary: https://www.gartner.com/en/information-technology/glossary/user-provisioning

Gordon, A. (2015). *Official (ISC)2 Guide to the CISSP CBK ((ISC)2 Press) 4th Edition.* Auerbach Publications.

Guide to International and Foreign Law Research. (n.d.). Retrieved from University of South Carolina School of Law: https://guides.law.sc.edu/c.php?g=315476&p=2108388

Harris, S., & Maymi, F. (2018). *CISSP All-in-One Exam Guide, Eighth Edition.* McGraw-Hill Education.

Herbane, B. (2010). The Evolution of Business Continuity Management: A Historical Review of Practices and Drivers. *Business History.*

INAP. (2017, May 10). *What is Business Continuity?* Retrieved from INAP: https://www.inap.com/blog/business-continuity/

ISACA. (2019). *Glossary.* Retrieved from ISACA: https://www.isaca.org/Pages/Glossary.aspx

ISO. (2000). *ISO 15704, Industrial automation systems — Requirements for enterprise-reference architectures and methodologies.* ISO.

ISO. (2009). *ISO/Guide 73:2009, Risk management — Vocabulary.* ISO.

ISO. (2013). *ISO 27001:2013, Information technology — Security.* ISO.

ISO. (2018). *ISO 27005:2018, Information technology — Security techniques — Information security risk management.* ISO.

ISO. (2018). *ISO 31000:2018, Risk management – Guidelines.* ISO.

ISO. (2019). *ISO 22301:2019, Security and resilience — Business continuity management systems — Requirements.* ISO.

ISO. (2020). *ISO 22313:2020, Security and resilience — Business continuity management systems — Guidance on the use of ISO 22301.* ISO.

Labarre, O. (2019, May 24). *Credit Risk.* Retrieved from Investopedia: https://www.investopedia.com/terms/c/creditrisk.asp

Laws and Regulations. (n.d.). Retrieved from U.S. Senate: https://www.senate.gov/reference/reference_index_subj ects/Laws_and_Regulations_vrd.htm

Massie, R. (2018, August 29). *What is Organizational Resilience?* Retrieved from The Business Continuity Institute: https://www.thebci.org/news/what-is-organizational-resilience.html

NIST. (2006, October). *Information Security Handbook: A Guide for Managers.* Retrieved from CSRC: https://csrc.nist.gov/publications/detail/sp/800-100/final

NIST. (2008, October). *Security Considerations in the System Development Life Cycle*. Retrieved from CSRC: https://csrc.nist.gov/publications/detail/sp/800-64/rev-2/archive/2008-10-16

NIST. (2010, May). *Contingency Planning Guide for Federal Information Systems*. Retrieved from CSRC: https://csrc.nist.gov/publications/detail/sp/800-34/rev-1/final

NIST. (2011, March). *Managing Information Security Risk: Organization, Mission, and Information System View*. Retrieved from CSRC: https://csrc.nist.gov/publications/detail/sp/800-39/final

NIST. (2012, September). *SP 800-30 Rev. 1, Guide for Conducting Risk Assessments*. Retrieved from CSRC: https://csrc.nist.gov/publications/detail/sp/800-30/rev-1/final

NIST. (2013, April). *Security and Privacy Controls for Federal Information Systems and Organizations*. Retrieved from CSRC: https://csrc.nist.gov/publications/detail/sp/800-53/rev-4/final

NIST. (2016, November). *Systems Security Engineering: Considerations for a Multidisciplinary Approach in the Engineering of Trustworthy Secure Systems*. Retrieved from CSRC: https://csrc.nist.gov/publications/detail/sp/800-160/vol-1/final

NIST. (2018, August). *Guide for Mapping Types of Information and Information Systems to Security Categories*. Retrieved from

CSRC: https://csrc.nist.gov/publications/detail/sp/800-60/vol-1-rev-1/final

NIST. (2018, December). *Risk Management Framework for Information Systems and Organizations: A System Life Cycle Approach for Security and Privacy.* Retrieved from CSRC: https://csrc.nist.gov/publications/detail/sp/800-37/rev-2/final

NIST. (2019). *NIST CSRC Glossary.* Retrieved from NIST CSRC: https://csrc.nist.gov/glossary

OCEG. (2019). *Governance, Risk and Compliance (GRC).* Retrieved from OCEG: https://www.oceg.org/about/what-is-grc/

Open Risk Manual contributors. (2019, November 6). *Risk Taxonomy.* Retrieved from Open Risk Manual: https://www.openriskmanual.org/wiki/index.php?title=Risk_Taxonomy&oldid=10517

PMI. (2017). *A Guide to the Project Management Body of Knowledge.* Project Management Institute.

PMI. (2019). *Project Management Institute.* Retrieved from PMI Lexicon of Project Management Terms: https://www.pmi.org/pmbok-guide-standards/lexicon

Presidential directive. (2019, July 13). Retrieved from Wikipedia: https://en.wikipedia.org/wiki/Presidential_directive

Project Management Institute. (2017). *The Standard for Program Management.* Project Management Institute.

Rittenberg , L., & Martens, F. (2012, January). *Enterprise Risk Management - Understanding and Communicating Risk*

Appetite. Retrieved from
https://www.coso.org/Documents/ERM-Understanding-and-Communicating-Risk-Appetite.pdf

Robeco. (2020, January 25). *Sustainable Investing Glossary.*
Retrieved from https://www.robeco.com/me/key-strengths/sustainability-investing/glossary/esg-definition.html

Spacey, J. (2017). *3 Examples of a Risk Profile.* Retrieved from
https://simplicable.com/new/risk-profile

TechTarget. (2007, June). *What is enterprise architecture (EA)?*
Retrieved from TechTarget Network:
https://searchcio.techtarget.com/definition/enterprise-architecture

Warsinske, J., Graff, M., Henry, K., Hoover, C., Malisow, B.,
Murphy, S., . . . Vasquez, M. (2019). *The Official (ISC)2
Guide to the CISSP CBK Reference 5th Edition.* Wiley.

Wikipedia. (2019). Retrieved from https://en.wikipedia.org/

Wikipedia. (2019, December). *Crisis management.* Retrieved from
Wikipedia:
https://en.wikipedia.org/wiki/Crisis_management

Made in the USA
Middletown, DE
13 December 2020